Spiritual Gifts

*Discover Joy!
by developing your spiritual
gifts for ministry.*

*A Grandmother's Legacy to Her Grandchildren
By Victoria Harr*

All Scripture quotations, unless otherwise specified, are taken from the King James Version of the Bible. (Copyright © 1982 by Holman Bible Publishers. All rights reserved.)

Scripture quotations noted NKJV are from the *Holy Bible*, New King James Version, (Copyright © 1979, 1980, 1982 by Thomas Nelson, Inc. Used by permission. All rights reserved.)

Scripture quotations noted NASB are from the *Holy Bible*, New American Standard Bible, (Copyright © 1960, 1962, 1963, 1968, 1971, 1972, 1973, 1975, 1977, 1995 by The Lockman Foundation. Used by permission. All rights reserved.)

Scripture quotations noted NIV are from the *Holy Bible*, New International Version, (Copyright © 1973, 1978, 1984 by International Bible Society. Used by permission.)

Scripture quotations noted NLT are from the *Holy Bible*, New Living Translation, (Copyright © 1996. Used by permission of Tyndale House Publishers, Inc., Wheaton, Illinois 60189. All rights reserved.)

Spiritual Gifts

By Victoria Harr

Copyright © 2006 by Victoria Harr

Published by
Vision Publishing
1115 D Street
Ramona, CA 92065
760-789-4700
www.visionpublishingservices.com
Printed in the United States of America

ISBN 1-931178-25-9

All rights reserved solely by the author. The author guarantees all contents are original and do not infringe upon the legal rights of any other person or work. No part of this book may be reproduced in any form without the permission of the author. The views expressed in this book are not necessarily those of the publisher.

Most scripture quotations, unless otherwise indicated, are taken from the King James Version.

SPIRITUAL GIFTS

DEDICATION

This letter is dedicated to my grandchildren whom I have not been able to influence spiritually as much as I did my children, due to geographical, time, and health restraints. It is my heart-felt prayer they will discover and use their spiritual gifts early in life. At the time of this writing, my two oldest grandchildren have accepted Jesus as their Savior and are in their late teens, so I am using Christian-ese terminology a lot of the time.

As I grew up, I found the King James Version (KJV) to be extremely rich, yet some words are archaic. Because of my gift of teaching, I was personally challenged to delve deeper into the meaning of certain words. Yet I realize that the younger generations find KJV hard to understand. Therefore, I have also quoted other versions and translations. Biblical quotes without a reference means I quoted KJV. Biblical quotes in bold indicate that I added an emphasis.

TABLE OF CONTENTS

Chapter   Page No.

Section 1
OVERVIEW OF ALL SPIRITUAL GIFTS

1	Love--The Fruit that Bears on All the Spiritual Gifts	5
2	My Baby Steps	7
3	First Things First	9
4	Purposes of the Spiritual Gifts	11
	Who Gets the Gifts?	
	Why?	
	For How Long?	
	Which Gifts?	
5	What Spiritual Gifts Are NOT!	13
6	Categorizing the Spiritual Gifts	15
7	Continuing the Journey	21

Section 2
MANIFESTATIONAL GIFTS

8	Definition of the Manifestational Gifts	25
	I Corinthians 12:4-11	
9	Definition of the Miscellaneous Manifestational Gifts	57
	I Corinthians 7:7 and Matthew 19:12	

Section 3
MOTIVATIONAL GIFTS

10	Definition of the Motivational Gifts	67
	Romans 12:6-8	
11	Motivational Gift Survey	77
	Instructions	78
	Scoring Sheet	79
12	Comparing and Contrasting the Motivational Gifts	87

Section 4
MINISTRY GIFTS

13	Definition of the Ministry Gifts	91
	Ephesians 4:11-12 and I Corinthians 12:28-30	
14	Conclusion	95

INTRODUCTION

After more than thirty years of learning, studying, teaching, and observing the demonstration, or lack of, the spiritual gifts in **non**-Pentecostal and **non**-charismatic churches, I believe the Holy Spirit has prompted me to write this letter so He will not continue to be quenched and grieved in His churches by individuals because of fear of the unknown, ignorance, lack of teaching, bad experiences, or other similar experiences. In reality, this is a letter about my personal journey. I have witnessed the abuse of the gifts in some of the charismatic churches. I have also observed that the gifts in most evangelistic, fundamental churches are not even recognized or acknowledged. Eventually I experienced the exercise of the gifts in a balanced, orderly, scriptural manner.

Most non-Pentecostal and non-charismatic churches do not emphasize teaching the spiritual gifts. These are supernatural gifts given by the Holy Spirit to a believer. I am convinced the majority of Christians, who are not brought up with teaching and experiencing them from the beginning of their Christian life, when challenged later by any of these gifts, will either shrink back from learning about them or be very hungry to learn more. I have noticed that this is a topic that is accompanied by a lot of curiosity, but when people begin to pursue the spiritual gifts, they often hit a stone wall in some form or other. They either have a bad experience, or they've heard of someone else who has had a bad experience. Either fear or poor self-esteem sets in, or they are simply not encouraged to discover and exercise their gifts. It is sad to me, because it grieves and quenches the Holy Spirit, causing that individual to lose an opportunity to know more of Jesus and what He is like. The Holy Spirit is a person, not an "it." When He is quenched, His holy fire is put out, and He is not able to work among His people. When He becomes grieved, He is sad. The end result is that believers will lack a lot of the power needed to live the victorious Christian life.

My observation has been that God takes us where we are in life and gives us gifts that emerge and develop according to His Sovereign plan. Sovereign means being in supreme control. As we're obedient and become more at ease with the Holy Spirit Himself, He adds those gifts we are more wary of or those we don't naturally lean to. For example, the gift of prophecy is a vocal gift, and I am naturally a vocal person. Therefore, I'm at ease with it, although God astounds me every time He uses me that way. However, when God puts me in a situation where mercy is called for, since I am not naturally a merciful person, often I struggle with being immediately obedient. The gift of mercy is one I need to develop through prayer.

I have walked with the Lord for over fifty years now. The first fifteen years of my Christian life I did not know there even was such a thing as spiritual gifts. Once I read about them directly from the Lord's Word, was formally taught about them, and then coupled that with my life's experiences, I had a whole change of perspective as to how I fit into the Kingdom of God. I deeply desire that all Christians experience their unique spiritual gifts and the joy that comes from using them for God's glory in ministry (service to God and others), so they may receive all God has for them. My heart's longing agrees with Paul who said in I Corinthians 12:1: "Now concerning spiritual [gifts], brethren, I would not have you ignorant." ("Brethren" includes both male and female Christians.)

Paul didn't want Christians to be ignorant of at least six things:

1. Spiritual gifts (I Corinthians 12:1);
2. Paul's apostleship (I Corinthians 14:38);
3. Baptism of the Israelites, pointing to baptism of the believer (I Corinthians 10:1-2);
4. Paul's trials (II Corinthians 1:8);
5. Satan and his devices and schemes, especially unforgiveness (II Corinthians 2:10-11); and
6. Second coming of Jesus (I Thessalonians 4:13 and II Peter 3:8-10).

Since Paul included the topic of spiritual gifts up there with other important doctrines, I think it must be very important for us to study.

In I Corinthians 14:12, Paul says if you are "... zealous of spiritual gifts, seek that you may excel to the edifying of the church." Strengthening the church is another pretty good reason to study and seek after the spiritual gifts, don't you think?

SECTION 1

OVERVIEW OF ALL SPIRITUAL GIFTS

CHAPTER 1

Love--The Fruit that Bears on All the Spiritual Gifts

Let's start at the beginning--and that beginning is Love. "In the beginning God..." and God loved us first. He died on the cross in the person of Jesus and forgave our sins. But it is not until we realize we are sinners, and we accept His love and forgiveness, that by the power of the Holy Spirit we are born again. At the point of being born again, being saved, accepting Jesus into your heart, making a commitment to Jesus, or whatever terminology you use, you become a new person within and instantly receive the Holy Spirit and **also receive spiritual gifts**. Did you know that? Well, don't feel bad--I didn't either when I started my Christian journey. I thought at salvation a person received the Holy Spirit, forgiveness of sins, and assurance of going to heaven--period. I didn't know that the spiritual gifts were also a part of the salvation package.

Walking with Jesus is an adventure. We go through many seasons in life and in our Christian walk, but if we are open to being changed from the inside out, more and more into His glorious image, we cannot help but be confronted by God about our many biases. It is at this time we can make a choice to continue to be safe in our present knowledge of Him or be stretched a little at a time to see what else He has to offer us.

As a new Christian there are so many things to learn, and often discovering our spiritual gifts doesn't seem to be a priority. I have observed that as time passes by, most Christians do not receive any teaching on the spiritual gifts. Years go by and we settle in to our church home. We adapt to their priorities in teaching, perhaps at times availing ourselves of other ministries' tapes, outside speakers, radio ministries, and other Christian resources. We bring many of our biases from our prior non-Christian life into our Christian walk. It does not matter which church we make our home, we all have preconceived notions that continue to influence us. These biases can stunt us spiritually. Often studying and discovering spiritual gifts just does not happen.

I Corinthians 13 is commonly referred to as the Love Chapter. It is interesting to me that I Corinthians 13 stresses Love as being the greatest attribute God wants us to experience. It is sandwiched between I Corinthians 12 and 14, which emphasizes the spiritual gifts, and when not exercised in love, has the most potential to split families and churches. It's like the peanut butter that holds the sandwich together. The list of spiritual gifts in Romans 12:6-8 is also sandwiched between a teaching on being members of one Body (the universal church), by stressing unity in verses 4 and 5, and ends in admonitions about love and how to exercise that love in verses 9 to the end. Finally, in the list of gifts in Ephesians 4:11, the teaching before (verses 1-7) and after (verses 12-16), also stresses love and unity in the Body. Is it as obvious to you as it is to me that God is driving home a point?

Even though I Corinthians 12:31 says, "But covet earnestly the best gifts...." I believe the Holy Spirit is stressing that Love is the main **fruit** (attribute) we all need in our lives before we can operate "... decently and in order...." with the spiritual gifts (I Corinthians 14:40). The motive for all the spiritual gifts operating should be the **fruit** of Love.

I Corinthians 13:1-13, NKJV

Though I speak with the tongues of men and of angels, but have not love, I have become sounding brass or a clanging cymbal. And though I have [the gift of] prophecy, and understand all mysteries and all knowledge, and though I have all faith, so that I could remove mountains, but have not love, I am nothing. And though I bestow all my goods to feed [the poor], and though I give my body to be burned, but have not love, it profits me nothing. Love suffers long [and] is kind; love does not envy; love does not parade itself, is not puffed up; does not behave rudely, does not seek its own, is not provoked, thinks no evil; does not rejoice in iniquity, but rejoices in the truth; bears all things, believes all things, hopes all things, endures all things. Love never fails.

But whether [there are] prophecies, they will fail; whether [there are] tongues, they will cease; whether there is knowledge, it will vanish away. For we know in part and we prophesy in part. But when that which is perfect has come, then that which is in part will

be done away. When I was a child, I spoke as a child, I understood as a child, I thought as a child; but when I became a man, I put away childish things. For now we see in a mirror, dimly, but then face to face. Now I know in part, but then I shall know just as I also am known. And now abide faith, hope, love, these three; **but the greatest of these [is] love.**

Love always defeats Satan (the devil). Just think about it. For instance, if you are tempted to be angry against someone, but instead forgive them because God gives you His supernatural love, you have defeated Satan right at the door. Or, if you start gossiping and realize it is a sin and repent, Satan is defeated without getting a foothold in your life. The spiritual gifts are also tools to defeat Satan. As you understand how they operate, you will see how the fruit and gifts work together. It's not really either/or-- it's both/and.

The gifts of the Holy Spirit are given to us to glorify the Father and Jesus, (not ourselves or the Holy Spirit (John 16:13)) and to edify and establish the Body of Christ (His church), so we can promote His Kingdom. If the gifts are motivated by love in that order, you can see there is a cycle that works like this.

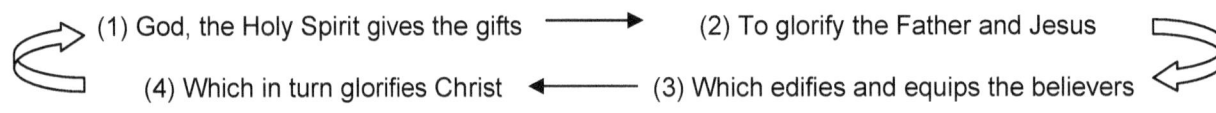

The spiritual gifts should not split churches or divide people by jealousy, envy, or other fleshly reactions. Sadly, historically in the churches, this has not been the case.

As you read through this letter, seek the <u>Giver</u>, not the <u>gift</u>. If you seek Jesus and really focus on Him, He will enhance your prayer life and give you the gifts as a by-product.

"Our influence finally depends upon our own experience of the unseen world and our experience in prayer. To influence, you must love. To love, you must pray."[1]

---

[1] Forbes Robinson, source unknown

CHAPTER 2

My Baby Steps

In my late twenties when the Lord began to reveal Himself to me personally, it was a whole new experience for me. I had attended a mainline denominational church since I was four years old, had been active in the youth group, had sung in the choir, and as an adult even served as a youth leader. Yet, I had never encountered the Lord in a way that could be described as supernatural, and I did not know you were supposed to. I had never been taught that this was a normal Christian's way to live, yet the Lord, in His mercy, sovereignly chose to reveal Himself to me through the spiritual gifts. Of course, I had no idea this is what they were called or (sad to say) even where to find them in the Bible. So God, in His mercy, directed me to a church with a pastor who was experiencing the same dynamics for the first time in his Christian walk.

Knowing what a practical person I am, God knew He had to reach me in supernatural ways I had never experienced before, so I would not doubt it was Him doing a work in me. Initially, I had no one to talk to who could answer any of my questions, so I went to the Bible for my answers. Now I realize it is preferable for everyone to go to the Bible for answers first, and let people be secondary sources. Because I didn't understand what was happening to me, sometimes I wondered if I was going crazy. But I wasn't--I just was learning a new aspect of the Holy Spirit.

The process went something like this. God would speak to me by an impression or thought that I knew wasn't mine, giving me a word or phrase to study, and I would go to His Word, the Bible. I would do a word search until I found the same words that would bear out that what He had said or shown me was true. This is how I learned what a concordance was and how to use it. At the very least, every layperson needs a concordance and a Halley's Bible Handbook to begin studying God's Word.

Sometimes I would be praying for solutions or answers to questions, and the Lord would impress an answer on my mind. I would go to the Word and find an example of that answer as a confirmation that it was Him speaking to me. Because I was such a spiritual baby and not that familiar with the Bible, it was strictly one miracle after another that helped me find the examples or words I needed to know. In this way I knew it was God, because I really didn't know where to look.

From time to time the Holy Spirit would speak to me symbolically or allegorically. I learned that if my understanding of what the Lord speaks to me seems out of context with the Biblical passage it came from, it is meant for me personally to build my faith. This kind of inspiration is for blessing--not doctrine.

Often when praying I would receive a specific insight about a situation that I had no way of knowing otherwise. Being new to this whole area, I would ask the Lord what it meant and what I was to do with that specific piece of knowledge. He would either speak directly into my heart or simply show me His answer as I was reading the Bible. If we seek out the answers in the Bible first and then go to people for confirmation, we will learn heart lessons that can never be taken away. In that way we will be able to pass those living lessons on to others.

Soon I realized a pattern was developing. I'd be talking to God (prayer) and would receive an answer either through a spiritual gift or while reading His Word. Sometimes I'd experience something totally out of the ordinary and go to the Word for validation. Either way, although I didn't know it, these experiences involved the spiritual gifts listed in I Corinthians 12 and 14.

At the same time, I began attending a women's Bible study in the book of I Corinthians. As we moved through the book verse-by-verse, I began to see that what was written there was happening to me on a frequent basis. The Bible became ALIVE to me for the first time. It was amazing to me to realize that God could reach down from heaven and communicate with me not only by His Word, but also by the Holy Spirit and through His gifts.

James 5:16(b), NKJV says, "The effectual fervent prayer of a righteous man avails much. Elijah was a man subject to like passions as we are and he prayed earnestly...." When I first began studying the Bible and became aware that it was alive, I read that verse and realized that I was just like Elijah. For the first time, I grasped the fact that as an ordinary person I had the same passions as everyone else, and therefore, I could zealously pray about any concerns I had and see the Lord answer in the same powerful way He answered Elijah's many prayers.

Soon after that, I began to systematically read through the Bible for the first time. I read about different characters in the Bible, and I started to study them. Of course, I knew all the Bible stories one hears in Sunday School about these characters, but studying the Word is different than reading the Word. I came to realize that if they experienced something, it could happen to me too. Those experiences are not limited to Biblical times, because God is not limited.

The Biblical characters of Elijah, Abraham, Moses, and the other prophets deeply influenced me as to how they talked to God and how He talked to them.

As I was reading the story of Abraham in Genesis 18:17 where the Lord said, "Shall I hide from Abraham that thing which I do; ...?"--that was when I decided to take God at His Word and ask Him to reveal things to me, to tell me what He had in store for me. As I have applied this verse about believing God will tell me things ahead of time, I have reaped the promise about my two children in verse 19, "For I know him, that he will command his children and his household after him, and they shall keep the way of the LORD, to do justice and judgment; that the LORD may bring upon Abraham that which he hath spoken of him."

As I continued to read, I discovered Exodus 33:11, NKJV "So the LORD spoke to Moses face to face, as a man speaks to his friend." I thought to myself, "Since God is the same yesterday, today, and forever, why wouldn't He talk to me face to face too?" I put that together with John 15:15, NKJV where Jesus says, "No longer do I call you servants, for a servant does not know what his master is doing; but I have called you friends; for all things that I heard from my Father I have made known to you." I decided right then and there that since I was considered a friend of Jesus, just like Abraham was a "friend of God," that must mean He would speak to me too, face to face (spiritually speaking) and guess what? He did. Soon I regularly applied this principle of listening to what He had to say, because He would talk to me-- not always, not immediately, but often enough for me to understand that I was to listen twice as much as talk to God. After all, that's why He gave us two ears and only one mouth, isn't it?

What I have studied and learned is scattered throughout this letter, alternating between sharing my personal experiences and actual teaching God has imparted to me which I have later used as a basis for teaching Bible studies to others.

CHAPTER 3

First Things First

I Corinthians 2:14, NKJV says, "But the natural man does not receive the things of the Spirit of God, for they are foolishness to him; nor can he know them, because they are spiritually discerned."

The natural man is not born again and doesn't receive or understand spiritual things. Only the man who is born again can receive and understand the spiritual gifts. If you try to operate by your natural temperament or in your natural strengths within the spiritual realm, it won't work, because it will be your own efforts.

Therefore, it is very important before we proceed that each of you knows you have received the Lord Jesus Christ as your personal Lord and Savior. If you haven't, here is a prayer to pray.

> Father God, in the name of Jesus, I want to tell You now that I have made the most important choice of my life. I acknowledge YOU are my God. I accept the truth that Jesus paid the price for all my sins on the cross. I acknowledge to you that I have done many wrong things. I am a sinner! I repent for those sins and ask you to forgive them and wash them all away with the precious blood of Jesus. Lord Jesus, I now make you my God, and I ask You to come into my heart and life by the power of the Holy Spirit. Change me Lord. Teach me to hear your voice and to live pleasing you. Please fill me with your Holy Spirit. I thank you God for accepting me and saving me, in the name of Jesus Christ.

If you were sincere in your prayer, then you are now headed for eternity with God--step by step, one day at a time. But don't stop here. God has so much more for you. So let's begin your adventure.

CHAPTER 4

Purposes of the Spiritual Gifts
Who Gets the Gifts?
Why?
For How Long?
Which Gifts?

Who gets the gifts? You do!

I Peter 4:10, NASB says, "As each one has received a [special] gift, employ it in serving one another as good stewards of the manifold grace of God." **Therefore, every Christian has received a spiritual gift to use for which they are accountable.**

Why? Paul wanted to impart to the believers in Rome a spiritual gift so they would be grounded in their faith and so their mutual faith would encourage him and each other.

Romans 1:11-12, NKJV says, "For I long to see you, that I may impart to you **some spiritual gift**, so that you may be established--that is, that I may be encouraged together with you by the mutual faith both of you and me." Those are marvelous reasons to ask for a spiritual gift, don't you think?

Purposes of the gifts: The spiritual gifts are ultimately given to us to (1) glorify Christ, and (2) edify and equip believers to grow and promote His Kingdom.

(1) <u>To glorify Christ</u>: "But when the Helper comes, whom I shall send to you from the Father, the Spirit of truth who proceeds from the Father, He will testify of Me" (John 15:26, NKJV).

"However, when He, the Spirit of truth, has come, He will guide you into all truth; for He will not speak on His own [authority], but whatever He hears He will speak; and He will tell you things to come" (John 16:13, NKJV).

Have you ever stopped to think what "glorify Christ" means in common laymen's terms? As Christians we throw that phrase around frequently, but do we really know what it means in a practical sense? To glorify Christ is to give him credit or honor for something He has done. When someone compliments me for something I did, I will say, "Thank you." If I know I did not do it in my own strength, I will say something along the lines of "It was the Lord," or "Thanks, but God prompted me [to say or do such and such]," or some such other answer that gives God the credit or honor He deserves.

(2) <u>To edify and equip believers to grow and promote His Kingdom</u>. To edify means to build up. "However, he has given each one of us a [special] gift according to the generosity of Christ." Why is it that He gives us these special abilities? So God's people will be equipped to do better work for Him, building up the church, the Body of Christ, to a position of strength and maturity "until we come to such unity in our faith and knowledge of God's Son that we will be mature and full grown in the Lord, measuring up to the full stature of Christ" (Ephesians 4:7 and 13, NLT).

For how long? Until Jesus returns.

I thank my God always concerning you for the grace of God which was given to you by Christ Jesus, that you were enriched in everything by Him in all utterance and all knowledge, even as the testimony of Christ was confirmed in you, so that you come short in no gift, eagerly waiting for the revelation of our Lord Jesus Christ, who will also confirm you to the end, [that you may be blameless] in the day of our Lord Jesus Christ (I Corinthians 1:4-8, NKJV).

Which gifts? God tells us in I Corinthians 12:31 that we are to covet earnestly the best gifts. That means to have a "warmth of feeling for." [1] Isn't that sweet to your heart? It is mine. He wants us to warmly desire the "best gifts" in each situation. I believe when he refers to the best gifts it means the gift that is needed the most for that moment. That's the best gift!

---

[1] *Strong's Concordance*, Copyright ©1979 by Thomas Nelson, Inc. Publishers. All rights reserved under International and Pan-American Convention.

CHAPTER 5

What Spiritual Gifts are NOT!

Before defining what spiritual gifts **are**, I think we need to define what they are **not**.

1. **Natural Talents and/or Learned Abilities vs. Spiritual Gifts.** Your natural or learned abilities or talents are not to be confused with your spiritual gift.

I have observed there is much confusion as people try to ascribe their natural abilities (such as an ability to organize well) or talents (like singing or playing an instrument) to spiritual gifts. Even unbelievers have talents and abilities given to them by God who is their Creator. They are not the same as the gifts of the Holy Spirit. To be sure, they are God-given abilities or strengths and are to be used to glorify God, but they are not **spiritual gifts**.

For example, Matthew 25:14-29 is the story of the servant who received a talent to invest, but who instead hid his talent. When the master returned, he was scolded for not investing his talent on the master's behalf so he could have earned interest. Verse 18 tells us these talents are money.

Except for where the word "talent" appears in Revelation 16:21, (meaning weight) all references to "talent" in the New Testament are to money.[1] Although our society uses the words talents and abilities interchangeably, the Bible does not. Therefore, talents in the Bible are never referred to as spiritual gifts.

2. **Natural Temperament and/or Personality vs. Spiritual Gifts.** Your natural temperament or personality is not to be confused with your spiritual gift. This is how God created you from before birth. Jeremiah 1:5, NIV says, "Before I formed you in the womb I knew **(or chose)** you, before you were born I set you apart; I appointed you as a prophet to the nations."

God also says in Isaiah 43:1, NKJV: "But now, thus says the Lord, who created you, O Jacob, and He who formed you, O Israel: 'Fear not, for I have redeemed you; I have called you by your name; You [are] Mine.'" And, again in verse 7: "Everyone who is called by My name, Whom I have created for My glory; I have formed him, yes, I have made him."

This indicates to me that one's temperament is formed in the womb.

When I was pregnant with my daughter, she was a placid baby to carry. She would occasionally roll over and change position just enough for me to know she was alive. During the entire nine months she didn't often awaken me during the night as many babies do. After she was born she continued to be a very placid child. Today her temperament is much the same. She takes life at a slower pace and is not an overly-energetic adult.

By contrast, while pregnant with my son, he was constantly active. He kept me from sleeping most nights. Even during the days, because he was always on the move, I was not comfortable. I felt like I was carrying a timpani drummer inside. From the time he was born he has always been on the move--active and rambunctious. As an adult he is that way now.

This is why I believe our temperament comes first. Later our environment and experiences will further affect our temperament and mold our personality.

3. **Gifts vs. Fruit.** People confuse spiritual **gifts** with spiritual **fruit**. There is a difference. **Fruit** is eternal and all Christians have **fruit**. **Gifts** are not eternal. Because Christians have all of the Holy Spirit residing within them, all Christians have all the **gifts**. However, not all Christians exercise all the **gifts**. Different **gifts** are exhibited in each believer as the Spirit directs, and the same gift can be demonstrated in a variety of ways as the Spirit chooses. These variations can differ within the same person or vary between people. To the extent one has the **fruit** of the Spirit in one's life is the extent to which the **gifts** can be exercised in an orderly, mature manner.

There are some Biblical words used to describe both fruit and gifts, but they have a different function.

---

[1] *Strong's Concordance*

The different characteristics of the **fruit** of the Spirit are found in three lists: Galatians 5:22-23, Ephesians 5:9, and Colossians 3:12-15.

Galatians 5:22-23, NASB says, "But the fruit of the Spirit is love, joy, peace, patience, kindness, goodness, faithfulness, gentleness, self-control: against such there is no law." Ephesians 5:9, NKJV says, "For the fruit of the Spirit [is] in all goodness and righteousness and truth."

Colossians 3:12-15, NKJV says:

Therefore, as [the] elect of God, holy and beloved, put on tender mercies, kindness, humility, meekness, longsuffering; bearing with one another, and forgiving one another, if anyone has a complaint against another; even as Christ forgave you, so you also [must] do. But above all these things put on love, which is the bond of perfection, and let the peace of God rule in your hearts, to which also you were called in one body; and be thankful.

The primary passage of scripture most commonly known to describe love is I Corinthians 13:1-13, which I have already quoted. This is a description of the **fruit** love, often called agape'.

Faith is also listed in I Corinthians 13:13 as **fruit** of the Spirit and is not a spiritual gift here or in Galatians 5:22-23 mentioned above.

II Corinthians 8:7, NKJV says, "So we urged Titus, that as he had begun, so he would also complete this grace in you as well. But as you abound in everything--in faith, in speech, in knowledge, in all diligence, and in your love for us--[see] that you abound in this grace also."

Paul is talking to the Corinthian church about giving and stressing that they abounded in EVERYTHING, and that he wants them to abound in giving also. It is the same today. He was speaking about the **grace** of giving, which is the same as the **fruit** of giving and is a command for all of us to learn to implement. However, the **gift** of giving is above and beyond this command and is given to some believers as a **motivational** gift. Many Christian leaders refer to the list of gifts in Romans as being **motivational** spiritual gifts. Why? Because I Peter 4:10, NASB says, "... **employ it in serving** one another...." **How** you employ it (are motivated to make use of it) determines the **way** you minister (serve).

In summary I believe:
1. We're **created** with a special temperament in the womb that is further affected by our environment and experiences--especially throughout our younger years, so our **interests** can act as vehicles for gifts, but are not spiritual gifts.
2. We're also **born** with natural talents.
3. We **learn** skills/abilities. A **talent or learned ability** is used in the non-Christian working world and may be used in the Body of Christ.
4. We receive the Holy Spirit and the gifts of the Holy Spirit when we are born-again. A **spiritual gift** works primarily in the Body of Christ. As you read the following definitions you will see why they are Body of Christ oriented. Some spiritual gifts are used more in the secular world (such as evangelism). Others are used primarily in the Church and secondarily in the secular world (such as prophecy).
5. All Christians have the **fruit** of love, which is eternal.
6. The **gifts** are temporary, for use until Jesus returns, and God decides how the gifts are to be distributed among and manifested in each person.

Now we are ready to continue not only learning about the spiritual gifts, but appropriating them. Remember, you must be filled with the Holy Spirit for the gifts to operate. To be filled means simply asking Jesus for His love and then believing in faith you have received it. Sometimes you will feel filled, and sometimes no feelings will be apparent, but if you step out in obedience, He will meet you. We can never predict exactly how God will meet us each time, but He will.

CHAPTER 6

Categorizing the Spiritual Gifts

I have been involved in several churches over my lifetime and have observed church splits in four of them over the spiritual gifts. This not only grieves the Holy Spirit, it creates wounded Christians and sometimes causes Christians to fall away. The communal ministry where I was involved **lived** the spiritual gifts--that is, they lived a spirit-filled lifestyle 24/7. As a group of believers, we did most things together, and because of the close quarters, we sandpapered each other. Repentance was a regular practice, and restoration was on-going. The ministry was evangelistic, so when people came to the Lord, their immediate exposure to the spiritual gifts was one of being the normal Christian life. As a result, God bestowed His gifts on brand new believers. However, in the churches I belonged to that were already established along main-line denominational lines where this was not a lifestyle during the week as well as on Sundays, whenever the pastor introduced the spiritual gifts to His flock, there would be skepticism, fear, and usually a split. I could not understand why that would happen. Although I had a burden to circumvent it, I was powerless to see how it could be avoided short of God's supernatural intervention.

So, for years I taught Bible studies on the spiritual gifts **combining them all together**, because that is how the Lord initially introduced them into my life. It was not until twenty-two years later that I was introduced to another way of approaching the spiritual gifts by categorizing them like the Bible does. For the first time it made sense to me why so many pastors seem to resist teaching the gifts and why so many Christians are therefore unable or afraid to embrace this part of their walk.

Although there are many ways to approach the study of the spiritual gifts and how to categorize them, I discovered that breaking them down the same way the Bible does makes it less divisive in a church or between individuals. I saw first-hand that when people object to teaching about or encouraging the use of the spiritual gifts, the first thing that typically happens is a division between those relationships or churches. It is sad that agape' (God's love) cannot prevail at this point. If Satan can get a toehold at the very beginning in an individual about even learning about the spiritual gifts, then he has won a victory by causing the Body of Christ to be divided. I pray that this letter will not only help you overcome any apprehension you might have regarding this subject, but that it will not be a cause for division in any area of your life.

God gives us the spiritual **gifts** primarily in three lists, just like He gives us three lists of the **fruit** of the Spirit. Some **gifts** and **fruit** are also scattered individually throughout scripture, as well. For the purposes of this letter, I have found the most logical way to approach this study is to categorize the gifts in three ways, because this is the way God has set them down for us. I will call the three categories of spiritual gifts, the **motivational** gifts, the **ministry** gifts, and the **manifestational** gifts. A **motivational** gift is the basic inward drive and ability that God places in each Christian. **Ministry** gifts are various opportunities of Christian service which are open for us to exercise our spiritual gifts. **Manifestational** gifts are special manifestations (evidences) that take place in and through the believer by the working of the Holy Spirit. These will be more fully described later.

The three specific categories of gifts of the Holy Spirit are found in Romans 12:6-8, Ephesians 4:11-12, and I Corinthians, Chapters 12:8-10 and 28. These gifts can also be observed in action as you read about accounts of individuals throughout the Gospels and Acts. The following chart will help you identify the gifts by their lists more readily.

Chart of Categories of Spiritual Gifts

Motivational Gifts	Ministry Gifts	Manifestational Gifts
The basic inward drive and ability that God places in each Christian.	The various opportunities of Christian service which are open for us to exercise our spiritual giftedness.	Special manifestations (evidences) that take place in and through the believer by the working of the Holy Spirit.
(Different Kinds of Gifts) I Corinthians 12:4 Romans 12:3-8	(Different Ministries) I Corinthians 12:5, 27-28 Ephesians 4:11-12	(Different Activities) I Corinthians 12:6-11 I Corinthians 12:28

Prophecy
Serving*
Teaching
Exhortation
Giving
Leadership**
Mercy
	Apostles
	Prophets
	Teachers
	Miracles
	Gifts of Healings
	Helps
	Governments/Administration
	Tongues
	Pastor/Teachers
	Evangelists
		A Word of Wisdom
		A Word of Knowledge
		Faith
		Gifts of Healings
		Working of Miracles
		Prophetic Utterances
		Discerning of Spirits
		Various Tongues
		Interpretation of Tongues
		
		I Corinthians 7:7-8 and Matthew 19:12
		    Eunuch/Singleness
		
		Joel 2:28-29 and Acts 2:17
		Genesis 37:5-11
		Daniel 7-8
		Matthew 1:20-21 and 27:19
		Acts 10:9-end
		    Dreams, Visions, and Interpretations of Dreams and Visions

* Some translations use helps. ** Some translations use ruling, administrative, or organization.		

Now, if you even have the slightest inkling you don't have a spiritual gift, don't entertain that thought any longer. Many believers fall into this trap of unbelief. Let me ask you: How much of the Holy Spirit did you receive when you were born again? Didn't you receive ALL of the Holy Spirit? Or did you only receive part of Him? I'm being facetious now. Of course you received ALL of the Holy Spirit. Did you know the spiritual gifts are also called the gifts of the Holy Spirit? When you received the Holy Spirit, He also arrived on the scene with His gifts. There are no second-class citizens in God's Kingdom, and He does not play favorites. Acts 10:34 says, "... God is no respecter of persons." Ephesians 6:9 repeats this idea. I personally believe since you received **all** of the Holy Spirit upon salvation, you also received ALL of the spiritual gifts. However, you probably will not experience all of them at once, because the Body of Christ is to work together as a team. No one is to be a lone ranger. Of course, if there is a need, you can be sure God is going to be there with an answer, and it may come in the form of any of the gifts. Your responsibility is to be open for the Master's use.

In the first list, Romans 12:6-8, NLT refers to seven spiritual gifts and how they are to be exercised.

> God has given each of us the ability to do certain things well. So if God has given you the **ability to prophesy**, speak out when you have faith that God is speaking through you. If your gift is that of **serving** others, serve them well. If you are a **teacher**, do a good job of teaching. If your gift is to **encourage** others, do it! If you have **money**, share it generously. If God has given you **leadership ability**, take the responsibility seriously, and if you have a gift for **showing kindness** to others, do it gladly.

When you are born again, the Holy Spirit enters your heart and you receive the gift of the Holy Spirit, including all His gifts. This means He makes you spiritually alive and begins to grow in you at least one **motivational** spiritual gift. Of these seven **motivational** spiritual gifts, one will be your **primary motivational** gift. God will give you **prophecy, service, teaching, exhortation, giving, leadership (ruling in KJV), or mercy**. Isn't that great news! This gift is the primary one you receive from the Holy Spirit when you are saved or born again, not when you're born. I Peter 4:10, NLT says, "God has given gifts **to each of you** from his great variety of spiritual gifts. Manage them well so that God's generosity can flow through you." Peter elaborates a little more about the gifts in verse 11. "Are you called to be a speaker? Then speak as though God himself were speaking through you. Are you called to help others? Do it with all the strength and energy that God supplies. Then God will be given glory in everything through Jesus Christ. All glory and power belong to him forever and ever. Amen."

Your **motivational** spiritual gift is the gift that **drives and motivates you and becomes your spiritual passion.**

Your **motivational** spiritual gift may enhance or be similar to your natural temperament, strengths, or abilities; or it may be completely opposite of your natural temperament, strengths, or abilities.

If your **motivational** spiritual gift is similar to your temperament or natural abilities, it will be harder to pinpoint your gift.

For example, if you are naturally outspoken and opinionated and the Lord gives you the gift of prophecy, you may not recognize it as a spiritual gift, because most people with this gift exercise it with a candid boldness in the Lord that may be mistaken for just being outspoken. The difference is--What are you outspoken about--Godly things or secular topics?

However, if your **motivational** spiritual gift is the opposite of your natural temperament or what you do naturally, then it may be very obvious to you. But, you still may feel awkward with its operation until you understand how it works.

On the other hand, if you are naturally a person who is not one to speak up unless specifically addressed, and the Lord gives you prophecy as a gift, it will be easier for you to recognize, because it will be such a contrast to your natural personality or temperament.

One clue is: If you can remember how you behaved and felt prior to becoming a Christian, it may be easier for you to recognize which of the seven gifts listed in Romans 12:6-8 God gave you when you were born again.

However, if you came to the Lord at an early age, it may be <u>harder</u> for you to separate your temperament from your **motivational** spiritual gift. I know many Christians who came to the Lord early in life, were raised in a Christian home and trained in the ways of the Lord, whose gift and temperament are similar. This made it harder for them to pick out their **motivational** spiritual gift from their Christian lifestyle.

Yet, you can be assured that everyone has at least one **motivational** spiritual gift, and you should be able to discover and recognize yours by the time you have finished this letter. Ephesians 4:7, NLT says, "However, he has given each one of us a **special** gift according to the generosity of Christ." Just remember--your special gift, your **motivational** spiritual gift, is the passion that drives you when relating to Biblical and/or spiritual matters.

The gifts in Ephesians 4:11 and I Corinthians 12:28 are referred to as **ministry** gifts, because the scripture says they are used "for the work of the ministry."

Ephesians 4:11, NLT gives us a second list of five spiritual gifts. "He is the one who gave these gifts to the church: the **apostles, the prophets, the evangelists, and the pastors and teachers**." Why? Verse 12 tells us it is "... their responsibility to equip God's people to do His work and build up the church, the Body of Christ." For how long? "... until we come to such unity in our faith and knowledge of God's Son that we will be mature and full grown in the Lord, measuring up to the full stature of Christ." Because this scripture describes a process which will take our lifetime, I believe all the gifts are active today and will be until Jesus returns.

In Ephesians 4, God sets out the **ministry** gifts of **apostles, prophets and teachers** which are repeated in I Corinthians 12:28 and then adds <u>more</u> **ministry** gifts as He has set in the church. These are **miracles, gifts of healing, helps, governments (administration in some translations), and tongues**. I believe any overlap seen within the lists is because God uses the same gift in different ways. For instance, some form of the gift of prophecy is found in all three lists. Because we are each unique individuals, the way each gift works in each individual is also unique. Examples of how this overlap might play out in an individual's life will be discussed later.

Finally, the third list consists of the **manifestational** gifts in I Corinthians 12. Paul begins with some instructions before listing these gifts. "Now concerning spiritual [gifts], brethren, I do not want you to be ignorant" I Corinthians 12:1, NKJV.

Paul continues in I Corinthians 12:4-11, NASB:

> Now there are varieties of gifts, but the same Spirit, and there are varieties of ministries, and the same Lord. There are varieties of effects, but the same God who works all things in all persons. But to each one is given the manifestation of the Spirit for the common good. For to one is given the **word of wisdom** through the Spirit, and to another the **word of knowledge** according to the same Spirit; to another **faith** by the same Spirit, and to another **gifts of healing** by the one Spirit, and to another the **effecting of miracles**, and to another **prophecy**, and to another the **distinguishing of spirits**, to another **various kinds of tongues**, and to another the **interpretation of tongues**. But one and the same Spirit works all these things, distributing to each one individually just as He wills.

The nine gifts above are referred to in different circles by various names: power gifts, sign gifts, revelatory, or charismatic gifts. However, for simplicity's sake, I will refer to this list of gifts as the **manifestational** spiritual gifts, because God says they will "manifest" (or exhibit) themselves when there is a need and you are willing to be used. It is then that God intervenes supernaturally.

Other **manifestational** gifts are found individually in various places in the Bible. Throughout Acts you will read about **dreams, visions, and interpretation of visions**. There are many characters in the Old Testament who had **dreams and interpretations of dreams**. The gift of **singleness** is discussed in I Corinthians 7:7 and Matthew 19:12.

When the spiritual gifts are sorted out this way, if a person has not studied the gifts, I think it is easier to understand how they can be discovered, demonstrated, and finally developed in the life of a believer in a non-divisive way. However, if you are puzzled at this point about how this all works together, don't worry. I was too, until I thoroughly studied this approach. It will be explained and developed more fully in Chapter 10, "Definition of the Motivational Gifts."

CHAPTER 7

Continuing the Journey

I accepted Jesus at age twelve, and until I was twenty-seven years old, I served him wholeheartedly by faith. It was mostly an obedient walk with sporadic points of joy, but I was not aware of anything of lasting power that touched others or multiplied His Kingdom. Mostly I just trudged along, aware that God loved me, knowing someday I'd get to heaven, but I didn't have much joy or peace accompanying my daily circumstances. Then God supernaturally touched me in such a way that I knew, that I *knew*, that **I knew** that Jesus was alive! Oh what a difference it made! Instead of being obedient and occasionally feeling joy, I was motivated by His love to be obedient. My perspective had completely changed. My cup overflowed with joy! It was then that I had something to give to others, and it was at that point God began to manifest Himself and the gifts of the Holy Spirit in power through me. Because the church I attended did not teach about the spiritual gifts, and I was experiencing a moving of the Holy Spirit in a new and different way, each time I recognized something God was doing in my life, I ran to His Word. I searched for an explanation in each situation I encountered, and for the first time, my prayer life became a conversational, personal two-way street--**talking and listening** to God. This is the fruit that abounds in a person's life once they begin to experience and recognize their gifts. It was at this time that I was becoming so secure in His love and acceptance of me, that I decided I wanted **all** God had to offer me, and I wasn't afraid of how that might look or feel. Every believer must come to this point of relaxing in God's arms, giving up their will for His will in their lives, no matter how it might look or feel, if they are to experience the power in their ministry that the Lord desires to give them.

Since I want to emphasize the part of my life in this letter that is my spiritual journey, I want to actually share about the **manifestational** gifts first. Although I was active in church beginning in my young childhood, I began to understand the **manifestational** gifts before I learned about the other gifts, because those were the ones that were happening to me in unanticipated ways. Chronologically I am going to relate the process the Lord used to teach me. He may teach you in a different way. Just be open to His Spirit.

To me, the **manifestational** gifts are the most exciting and rewarding part of my walk with Jesus. It can be yours too. They are probably the most exciting, because they are always an unexpected surprise from God. You never know when, how, or where the Holy Spirit will move. After all, Jesus compared the Holy Spirit to the wind in John 3:8, NKJV. "The wind blows where it wishes, and you hear the sound of it, but you cannot tell where it comes from and where it goes. So is everyone that is born of the Spirit." If you have not been filled with God's Spirit afresh, now would be the time to recommit yourself to Him so you can receive all He has for you.

Many times I have seen people who love the Lord, who are serving him wholeheartedly and where the **manifestational** gifts are operating in their lives, yet they do not even recognize or acknowledge their existence. How sad this is to me. This is another way people and churches get hung up with their biases. Some of it is from lack of teaching, and some of it is because of misunderstood expectations or just plain fear. When you are in ministry, you will be exposed to specific situations where God will send a **manifestational** gift to meet that need. These **manifestational** gifts will have a supernatural power, but they may not necessarily be overpowering in a physical sense. The Biblical test is: Did this gift bear fruit? That's where the true and lasting power lies. There is no need to be uneasy about these gifts--unless, of course, you are afraid of God and what He might do. To serve God is to relinquish your control in all areas, even in the area of spiritual gifts. If you are anxious about losing control in this area, then you should ask yourself why you don't trust God in relation to this.

Now let's look at what I mean by **manifestational** gifts.

SECTION 2

MANIFESTATIONAL GIFTS

CHAPTER 8

Definition of the Manifestational Gifts
I Corinthians 12:4-11

Manifestational Gifts: A momentary empowerment that takes place in and through a believer, by the working of the Holy Spirit, to meet a specific or immediate need or situation.

Now we come to the fun part, at least it is for me. You will discover a by-product of the **manifestational** gifts will not only be joy, but you may even experience unexpected exuberance or exhilaration in your spirit at times. As God changed my heart, I became more concerned with others. You will discover, through ministry to others, your own needs will take a back seat, and He will allow you to supernaturally experience the **manifestational** gifts.

When you exercise faith in any matter, there is a bit of an element of "what if" that seems to accompany a risk, isn't there? However, when the **manifestational** gifts begin to operate in your life and you recognize them, they also bring an element of fun. This is not meant to be disrespectful, but rather another dimension of God. He is not a stick in the mud kind of God, and walking with Him is not boring. These gifts are one way of experiencing another side of His nature. God has even demonstrated His sense of humor to me in many ways. Sometimes the way He works or what He says just cracks me up. The Bible illustrates many humorous examples.

An amusing story is found in Acts 12. Peter was in prison, and the local church was praying for his release. After an angel of the Lord freed him, he went out of the prison, past the guards, and through an iron gate. All the time Peter was thinking he was having a vision. Once he realized this was happening in real time, he went directly to the house where the prayer meeting was being held. He knocked at the gate, and the young lady who came to answer it saw it was him, but she got so excited that she ran back to the believers inside, leaving Peter standing outside. When she told them that Peter was at the door, they did not believe her. Here they were praying for him, probably praying for his release, and when he showed up, they didn't believe it! I think God was amused at how everyone reacted. How often do we pray for something, and when it happens we really don't believe it at first? I think God understands our foibles and at times has a sense of humor towards our ineptness.

When I was first introduced to these gifts in I Corinthians, I was in a Bible study at my church, and each week we learned about one gift. I would get so enthusiastic about this new way of walking in the Spirit, that I'd go home, and all week I'd pray for the gift we had just studied. Since Paul says in I Corinthians 1:7 that he wanted us to "come behind in no gift," and since I sure didn't want to fall behind in anything spiritually, I'd ask the Lord for that gift. Oh, that was surely the one I wanted above all others! Then the next week we would learn about the next gift and my prayer would change. That's the gift I wanted. They were all so wonderful; I couldn't make up my mind. I became as Joy Dawson says, "forever ruined for the ordinary."[1]

Somewhere along the line I learned that all of the gifts were mine for the asking, but it was up to God to bring them out in me as a need arose. Even though I continued to ask for all the gifts, I began **studying**, not just **reading** the Bible for myself, and I placed myself in positions of praying with others. That way if there was a need, I figured perhaps the Lord would use me to meet that need. Do you know what? Even if He used someone else, when they shared about an answered prayer, I was just as thrilled as if I'd been the vessel He'd used. During this time I began to have a heart for women that I'd never had before, and I also learned to rejoice with those that rejoice.

---

[1] Joy Dawson, *Forever Ruined for the Ordinary*, (Nashville: Thomas Nelson, 2001)

I Corinthians 14:12 says, if you are "zealous of spiritual gifts, seek that you may excel to the edifying of the church." The **manifestational** gifts bring much zeal with them. We always need to keep our priorities in line and be sure we are edifying the church and not just ourselves when they are operating. Matthew 12:39, NKJV says, "But He answered and said to them, 'An evil and adulterous generation seeks after a sign, and no sign will be given to it....'" Jesus is talking about the sign of him being in the earth three days and nights after his death, like Jonah was in the whale three days and nights. Even though in this context the "sign" does not refer to spiritual gifts, there is a spiritual principle here. In order for us to not have misplaced priorities, instead of chasing after signs (gifts), we need to run after Jesus. As we discover Him, He will give us signs in the form of gifts, but we should not make the gifts our primary focus.

Often the **manifestational** gifts seem to work in triplets. If you study Jesus' life and Acts, you will readily see that where one dominant gift is operating, two or three others will be operating as well. The gifts never seem to operate alone. You will see what I mean by the following stories I have lived through.

When observed in the New Testament stories, generally the gifts aren't specifically identified or labeled when practiced, but I am taking the liberty to identify certain gifts based on the circumstances surrounding its use.

Word of Wisdom

Definition: A supernatural revelation given by the Holy Spirit to a believer on how, when, where, and to whom to share timely knowledge of God's will, purposes, and plans.

I believe this gift is **not** wisdom gained by experience or age. I say this because I have experienced the Lord working this way in me, and I have observed it in others. The emphasis is on "word" more than emphasizing wisdom. A word of wisdom is wisely spoken words at the right time, to the right person, in the right place. It is the perfect solution. It is like "apples of gold in pictures of silver" (Proverbs 25:11). It may be a word meant exclusively for you, or it might be meant for someone else.

A word can be a phrase or sentence, just like theologians refer to Jesus' last seven words on the cross. They were not just words, but entire sentences. In the same way, the gift of a word of wisdom can also come in the form of a sentence, not just a single word.

In Acts 23:6-7, we see Paul speaking to the Sanhedrin Council.

> But when Paul perceived that the one part were Sadducees, and the other Pharisees, he cried out in the council, Men [and] brethren, I am a Pharisee, the son of a Pharisee: of the hope and resurrection of the dead I am called in question. And when he had so said, there arose a dissension between the Pharisees and the Sadducees: and the multitude was divided.

Once God showed Paul that there was a mixed crowd theologically speaking, he was able to cause enough doubt among them that they did not know what to do with him. As a result, we see in verse 10 that the chief captain returned him to the castle and to safety. The word of wisdom God gave Paul probably actually saved him from a beating or worse. God often works in our lives in such a natural way that we sometimes don't realize something supernatural is happening until after the fact.

When God began to reveal this gift to me, He did it in stages. I have confidence He will do that with you too, especially if you are as apprehensive or as unknowledgeable about the supernatural as I was. Initially I was the recipient of words from wise women who would speak into my life. I always marveled at their gentleness and timeliness in approaching me. Their words were "easily entreated" (as James says) by my Spirit. As I grew in the Word of God, He began to give me the gift of the word of wisdom to share with others. With the modeling I had observed, I always tried to approach others in this way. Since those years, through different churches, I learned it is a two-way street. Sometimes God sends someone to me with a **word for me**, and sometimes He sends me to another with a **word for them**. Either way, this is a wonderful gift!

Sometimes the person speaking a word of wisdom isn't aware God is using them unless the person receiving the word of wisdom acknowledges that fact. We should let the other person know when that word has pricked our hearts as this is a confirmation which encourages the one exercising the gift. It builds up the Body of Christ.

Recently, I felt I had a word of wisdom for a young man, and when I shared it with him, he confirmed it was what he was already considering. What I want to emphasize with the word of wisdom is that God's timing is always right on target.

Sometimes a word of wisdom is what is to be done with a word of knowledge previously given. The word of knowledge is the next gift we will discuss.

Word of Knowledge

Definition: To perceive, understand, feel, have, or be aware of a fact that comes to you supernaturally that you would have no way of knowing otherwise.

Because of what I have observed and experienced I believe this gift is **not** knowledge gained by book learning. It is not knowledge acquired in general. It is a perfect solution **without previous facts** as to an exact person or a specific situation. Again the emphasis is on **word.**

A perfect example would be in John 4:5-29--the story of Jesus and the Samaritan woman. Jesus knew all about her, and in declaring his knowledge of her past to her, she initially perceived that he was a prophet.

Sometimes the word of knowledge may come in the form of a phrase in a song. It may manifest itself in a single word or piece of information about someone or something. Remember, we serve a God of variety. We can't limit how or the way He gives gifts. This gift often works together with a word of wisdom. Sometimes a word of knowledge needs the word of wisdom for its proper application. You may understand how to apply it much later after you've had time to talk to God about it.

Because this gift is actually God speaking directly to you on a certain matter, it may often be a puzzlement to you. It may be only for you, or it may be for someone else. You should ask God if this word applies to you first--most of the time it will. Ask Him if this word of knowledge might also be for someone else. Then ask for guidance as to whether or not it is to be shared with that person or just kept to yourself. Often words are not to be shared with anyone, not even the other person, but are for your information only as a matter of prayer.

I have a Holy Spirit shelf. Well, of course, it's not really a shelf. It's just where I spiritually store the information I receive. Whenever I receive a word of knowledge or a prophecy that I do not understand, I ponder it in my heart (like Mary did when the angel came to her and told her about bearing Jesus). After prayer, if I still lack specific wisdom as to what to do with that word of knowledge or prophecy, I put it out of my mind and put it on my Holy Spirit shelf. By faith and by having experienced this numerous times, I know that when the time is right, God will bring it to my mind and shed more light on it. I don't try to figure it out. If He wants me to know more or do something about it, He will let me know. Until then my role is to pray and rest in Him. This is often hard to do, because our natural mind wants to figure everything out, but if you just wait on Him, your blessing will be complete. If you rush into a situation without wisdom, you could create a bit of a mess and miss a blessing.

Just as with the word of wisdom, the person speaking a word of knowledge may not be sure that this word is from God unless the person receiving the word of knowledge acknowledges that fact. We should let the other person know when that word has pierced our hearts as a confirmation to them. It will help their faith grow as well as yours.

Philip shows us a good example of the word of knowledge and the word of wisdom being exercised in Acts 8:26-33, NIV. He had been instructed by the Lord to go to the Gaza desert. This was a word of knowledge. There he met an Ethiopian eunuch returning from worshipping in Jerusalem. As the eunuch was reading Isaiah, the Spirit told Philip to overtake his chariot. This also was a word of knowledge. Being prompted by the Spirit, Philip asked him "Do you understand what you are reading?" This word of wisdom was the perfect question to open up a conversation so Philip could explain the scriptures to him. The result was that Philip shared Jesus with the Ethiopian, and later he was baptized.

Acts 5:1-11, NLT is another account where Peter was exercising the gift of the word of knowledge and the word of wisdom. Ananias and his wife Sapphira had sold a piece of land, but he kept back part of the proceeds, and his wife knew about it. They brought part of the money and laid it at the apostles' feet. But Peter said:

> Ananias, why has Satan filled your heart to lie to the Holy Spirit and keep back part of the price of the land for yourself? While it remained, was it not your own? And after it was sold, was it not in your own control? Why have you conceived this thing in your heart? You have not lied to men but to God.

God had given Peter a word of knowledge and a word of wisdom for Ananias. Then "Ananias, hearing these words, fell down and died." He was carried out and buried. About three hours later his wife came in, not knowing what had happened, and Peter asked her, "Tell me whether you sold the land for so much?" She said, "Yes, for so much." Then Peter said to her, "How is it that you have agreed together to test the Spirit of the Lord? Look, the feet of those who have buried your husband are at the door, and they will carry you out." Once again, God had given Peter a word of knowledge and a word of wisdom, but this time it was for Sapphira. Verse 10 says, "Instantly, she fell to the floor and died. When the young men came in and saw that she was dead, they carried her out and buried her beside her husband. Great fear gripped the entire church and all others who heard what had happened." Obviously you can see this is a powerful gift and must be used wisely.

Whenever I hear from the Lord, whether through a word of knowledge or a prophecy, I immediately run it through a grid of testing:

1. Is this scriptural? (Does it line up with God's character and/or is there a scripture that applies to it?)
2. Does this apply to me? (It may be for you only.)
3. Does it apply to someone else? (It may have a double application for both you and someone else.)

When I was in my twenties, I was being led by the Lord to move from California to join a ministry in Oregon called Shiloh. I had never been out of California nor had I ever visited that ministry. I knew the Lord wanted me to move, but I had no idea how it would look. As a woman traveling with two young children, I was hesitant to get in my car with all my belongings and just hit the road. I mulled this over, but couldn't come up with a solution, so I temporarily set it aside. One day I heard the phrase "I will give you a police escort from California." This was a word of knowledge, but I had no understanding (no word of wisdom) to go with it, so I laughed, just like Abraham's wife, Sara. I couldn't imagine how that would happen or if it really was from the Lord, but with that word came a peace, and I was no longer apprehensive about the long drive to Oregon. Over the next six months I shared my plans with many people and received some good counsel. One couple I had known for years were absolutely delighted for me and jumped at the chance to help me pack. They even offered to caravan up to Oregon with my family. Of course, I saw it as the Lord's protection and provision--I'd have company and others with me if I had car trouble, so we proceeded as planned. It was a two-day trip, including an overnight stay. After arriving in Eugene, I checked into their ministry headquarters, we unloaded my car and their camper and went to the communal kitchen to eat dinner. It was not until we all sat down and gave thanks for the safe trip that the Lord brought back that phrase to me "I will give you a police escort from California." I looked across the table and suddenly the "lights came on." The husband of the couple was a police office on temporary disability leave. I had not even put those facts together until then. I shared with them for the first time right then what the Lord had told me six months earlier. We all had a good laugh as we recognized the Lord's ways are not our ways. Can you see how the Lord will bring His words to pass in His timing, not ours? We don't have to dwell on what it might mean, because He will reveal an interpretation to us when we need it.

For a couple of years while I was part of that communal ministry, I lived in an apartment complex with eight other single moms on a street named McKinley. The apartment was paid for by the ministry. At one point, the elders wanted us all to move out and become more self-sufficient if possible, and we were given a flexible timeframe to find work. As each mother found jobs and bettered themselves, they began to move out into larger apartments or homes. I was looking for another apartment, but I was becoming anxious because I couldn't find anything in my price range, and everyone else had. Then the Lord told me I'd be "the last one out of McKinley." This was a word of knowledge, because it wasn't complete. It was very comforting and took the pressure off me as I watched five of them move out. Meanwhile, I had found a nice apartment and began packing. As moving day approached, there were still three of us in the complex. I had planned to move first thing in the morning, but the movers had scheduling problems. As it turned out, the other two single moms were out by noon, and I didn't get out until 4 PM, fulfilling that previous word. Only the Lord knew the exact timeframe of moving when He gave this insight to me weeks earlier. Now you might say "Well, that was a small thing, why would the Lord bother telling you that in advance?" My answer to that is--to me it was not a small thing. Worrying about finding another place to live and moving had the potential of occupying my thought-life to the exclusion of everything else. Once the Lord spoke to my heart, I didn't let the moving preparations distract me from being a good witness, even when I saw the others leave one-by-one. I had the "peace that passes all understanding," because I knew I was in the center of God's will. The unbelieving neighbors thought with my legal skills and experience I'd find a job first. Since I didn't, this is how I was able to witness to them as the Lord took me through the process. They were amazed at my confidence and peace in the midst of the unsettled situation. Yet, I knew it wasn't me--it was Jesus giving me the gifts of the word of knowledge and faith. The gift of faith is another gift we'll discuss later.

As I grew in exercising the word of knowledge and the word of wisdom individually, the Lord started giving me both at the same time. Then I began learning how to share those words in faith, believing it was the right word for the right person in the right situation. However, some people did not always acknowledge what I shared as having any meaning to them at the time. I've learned over the years, that most people (1) don't know how to affirm someone, or (2) they don't know how the word fits with them and their situation at the time, or (3) the word was on target, but they were embarrassed that someone else knew about it. I must admit it can be a shock if you share something with a person that only they and God know about. This is all the more reason to be sensitive when sharing with others.

Hebrews 10:31 says, "[It is] a fearful thing to fall into the hands of the living God." When these gifts operate, with or without prophecy, if you're not acting in love and meekness, it can scare people. It can make them feel as though you can read their mind or see through them, so humility is of utmost importance in exercising the gifts.

Whether or not the recipient recognizes it as a gift from God, more often than not I'm aware if it's a word of wisdom or a word of knowledge. This is partly due to experience in exercising those gifts and partly due to having the gift of discerning of spirits that we will study later.

There is also a process in developing your gifts. Just because you have a gift doesn't mean it is mature in its operation or growth. You grow as a person in the Lord, and the gifts grow as you develop too.

Faith

Definition: An unwavering persuasion, given in special measure or degree for specific instances; the ability to operate on an unusual level of faith for a period of time for a specific purpose or thing. This is not a denial of facts, but a belief that ultimately reveals results.

This gift of faith is **not** the same as **fruit** of faith described in Galatians 5:22, nor the **grace** of faith which occurs in most other instances in the New Testament, nor **saving** faith which is given to all believers and described in Ephesians 2:8 and I Peter 1:9. This gift causes you to stand on God's promises as revealed in the whole counsel of God. It could include believing things about which the Bible may be silent, but it doesn't contradict the Bible, and it produces results. Sometimes you are the only one who has been given this gift of faith for a certain situation. Others may see a natural potential in a person or situation, but when you have the gift of faith, you know that you know that you know. There is no permanent wavering. Even if Satan temporarily shakes that certainty you possess, when you seek the Lord again, the faith returns with an assurance beyond description.

In Acts 21:10-14, NKJV Paul was warned not to go to Jerusalem by a prophet, yet he had the gift of faith to go anyway and be bound up, even if it meant death. He was fully persuaded, because the Holy Spirit had revealed this to him in Acts 20:22-23. In this example, he was demonstrating what he later said in II Timothy 1:12, NJKV: "For this reason I also suffer these things; nevertheless I am not ashamed, for I know whom I have believed and am persuaded that He is able to keep what I have committed to Him until that Day."

When the gift of faith is given to someone, it comes as a paradox. On one hand, you have such assurance that you have indescribable joy or peace because you just know that God's promise to you in a particular situation is going to come to pass. On the other hand, it crucifies your natural fleshly tendencies because it is not usually forthcoming quickly. You may not see the fulfillment of it for years. I can promise you, you will learn patience with this gift.

I have observed this gift many times operating with the parent of a prodigal child knowing deep within that their child would return to their faith. I have also observed believers with this gift of faith that confidently declare to others that their unbelieving spouse will become a believer. By the same token, others observing those types of situations, not having the gift of faith, will not be so convinced.

Prior to my moving to Oregon, which I talked about before, during prayer the Lord gave me the word--"Shiloh." I had no clue what it meant. I had never even heard of Shiloh. After months of doing a word study through the Bible, and counseling with my pastor, I found out there was a ministry called Shiloh in Oregon which had a general evangelistic outreach, with a particular calling to single moms. As I learned more about it, and as the Lord continued to lead me in that direction, I knew that I was going to end up there. Why? I wasn't sure. When? I couldn't tell you. How? I had no idea. I owned a home, had two young children, a career, and had many loose ends to tie up--not to mention I was never led to visit that particular body of ministry ahead of time. By all outside appearances, I was not being very practical. I just knew that was where God wanted my children and me. It was very strange trying to explain to anyone that I was going to move to Oregon, but wasn't exactly sure of anything else. I got all kinds of strange reactions, but my faith grew, and I persevered in that direction as the Lord opened one door after another for over nine months. He gave me one scripture after another during that time, and the gift of faith grew in me. I cannot explain the joy I felt when it came to pass.

Acts 4:32, NKJV describes the gift of faith in action in the early church.

> Now the multitude of those who believed were of one heart and one soul; neither did anyone say that any of the things he possessed was his own, but they had all things in common. And with great power the apostles gave witness to the resurrection of the Lord Jesus and great grace was upon them all. Nor was there anyone among them who lacked; for all who were possessors of lands or houses sold them, and brought the proceeds of the things that were sold, and laid them at the apostles' feet; and they distributed to each as anyone had need.

Once I arrived at Shiloh, I saw the gift of faith in action in a way I'd never seen before or since, because this was a communal ministry which operated financially like the church described above. Upon committing ourselves to this ministry, we became part of the community's financial structure. We were not required to sell any personal items we previously owned, but we voluntarily shared clothes, food, cars, and financial resources out of love for the believers. Those who were single, worked and shared their entire income for the benefit of all the believers, so those who could not work still had their needs met. Everything was put into one "pot" and distributed as the needs arose. This required a lot of faith on everyone's part to believe all their necessities would be provided for.

As you step out in obedience in small things, you will receive more faith for bigger things. To me, moving to Oregon was a **big** step of faith, but it wasn't always that way with me. In the years before that, God gave me the gift of faith for smaller things, like money to meet my bills, food to feed my family, and many people to help meet other practical needs I had. I'd have a need, and after making my needs known to Him in prayer, the Lord would give me the gift of faith that He was going to provide. I never knew how, but each time He promised me something, the weight and any anxiety would be lifted, and the need would be met in an unexpected way. Just watching God work is exciting!

Gifts of Healing

Definition: The supernatural conveyance of God's healing power to provide a cure of some type to a person needing healing.

The gifts of healing can be (1) mental, (2) physical, (3) emotional, or (4) spiritual. This gift can be instantaneous, but not necessarily so. It can be in stages. The following examples will demonstrate how this gift may be received for your own healing or used for other people's healings.

This gift is the only one listed that says it is plural. Look at it again--gift**s** of healing. That tells me there are at least two ways of experiencing this gift. One way to experience this gift is as a <u>recipient</u> healed directly by God without any intervention from a third party. This would be a miraculous healing--one whose only explanation is God. As a <u>recipient</u> of a gift of healing, through prayer alone, you may receive many healings over your lifetime. The second way to experience this gift is as a <u>vessel</u>. As a <u>vessel</u>, you may have a healing ministry through prayer and/or laying on of hands, and God would use that ministry to cause a healing in others. As a <u>vessel</u>, the Spirit may use your calm demeanor so that when people are around you, they are comforted in such a supernatural way that it would lead them into accepting or receiving a healing. I knew a woman once who had just such a demeanor. When she spoke, it was quiet, but with authority. She would share the Word of God in such a way that being in her presence brought a "balm of Gilead" to a person or situation. More often than not, God also brought emotional and spiritual healing as well. I saw Jesus work through her, causing people who were agitated, confused, or disturbed to be soothed just by being with her. It was not anything she sought after--God just gave her the gifts of healing, which He developed into a very personal healing ministry.

Because this is a highly sought-after gift, we need to remember God is the Giver of the gifts, and the person exercising any gift has nothing apart from God. We have to be careful not to glorify a person or a gift, or think more highly of them or of ourselves. We have to watch out for pride. This is how I recognize pride. What's in the middle of pride? "I" is in the middle. We have to watch out for the "I" in all the gifts, and remember the Holy Spirit needs to be in the middle instead of "I."

The first category of healing is *mental*. Mark 5:1-20 tells us the story of Legion, "a man with an unclean spirit." No one could tame or bind him, even with chains, but when he saw Jesus, he ran and worshipped Him. Jesus said to him, "Come out of the man, [thou] unclean spirit!" When He asked him his name, he said, "... Legion; for we are many." When the village people "... came to Jesus, and saw the one who had been demon-possessed and had the legion, **sitting and clothed and in his right mind**, they were afraid."

I have personally known many young people coming out of the 1960's and '70's drug culture who were literally out of their minds because of drugs. They were unable to carry on a conversation with anyone, hold a job, or relate in any manner to reality. They were totally "out of it." Then they accepted Jesus, and God totally healed their minds. Sometimes they received salvation and later a healing, and sometimes both happened at the same time they accepted Jesus. They have become well-functioning individuals, able to contribute to society. Some are even well-known pastors today.

The gifts of healing may be dynamically apparent by virtue of the healing itself. Sometimes this gift is dramatically demonstrated when someone is healed. Sometimes it is not so dramatic. We should not seek emotionalism, but if someone is healed, emotions frequently accompany such a gift. After all, why shouldn't emotions be appropriate? If you've been in any kind of physical, mental, or emotional pain and are then set free from that pain, you'd probably be very amazed at the least. Your emotions could run the gamut.

Remember the lame man in Acts 3:1-1--walking, and leaping, and praising God? This was an example of both the second and third categories of healing--a *physical* healing-- "Immediately his feet and ankle bones received strength," (verse 7) and an *emotional* healing "And he leaping up stood, and walked, and entered with them into the temple, walking, and leaping, and praising God" (verse 8). I think it was both--not because he showed emotions by jumping around, but I think after all those years of being lame from birth and having to beg for alms daily at the temple gate, he must have been discouraged at the least--maybe even depressed or suicidal. He reacted emotionally, because he was physically healed. Why wouldn't he be emotional? His healing was manifested publicly, but some healings are manifested more privately. Some healings are confirmed medically, and that may take a little time. This gives us a chance to witness to the doctors, nurses, and others who were a part of the illness.

The fourth category of healing is *spiritual*. Acts 28:26-27, NKJV says:

Go to this people and say: 'Hearing you will hear, and shall not understand; and seeing you will see, and not perceive; for the hearts of this people have grown dull. Their ears are hard of hearing, and their eyes they have closed, lest they should see with their eyes and hear with their ears, lest they should understand with their hearts and turn, so that I should heal them'.

Every time someone is saved, they receive a spiritual healing. When someone is delivered from depression or demonic influence of some kind, it is also a type of spiritual healing.

You can receive gifts of healing over and over again for the same sickness or affliction. I know there are those who say when God heals it is complete the first time, but I have seen people healed from cancer for years by going into what man calls remission. They may live years without this disease rearing its ugly head again, or they may be completely healed all at once.

The gift of healing can be in stages. Mark 8:22-25 tells us about Jesus spitting on the blind man's eyes and putting his hands on his eyes. When the man looked up, he saw "men as trees, walking." He did not see perfectly the first time Jesus touched him, so Jesus touched his eyes again, and that time it says, "... he was restored, and saw every man clearly." Once again, this shows me we cannot limit the way God works.

One day God revealed to me that when it appears that God did not heal because the sickness remained the same, it could be because He did intervene just by virtue of the fact that the sickness didn't get worse. How are we to know for sure? Sometimes what looks like no healing is really Him sparing us from something we can't see. If we had not prayed for a healing, how do we know it would not have become worse? I do not believe you can be dogmatic about the gifts of healing.

As a general rule, no two gifts of healing are alike. Sometimes physical feelings are present, but not always. God uses these feelings as confirmation to the person being healed or as confirmation to increase faith on the part of those involved. Healing may involve laying on of hands, but it doesn't have to.

The gift of healing can also occur without any faith on your part. The person being healed doesn't necessarily have to have faith if he has friends who do. Look at Mark 2:1-12. Jesus was in a house in Capernaum, and the word was out that healings were happening. His friends brought an unnamed man, sick with the palsy, to Jesus. We do not see any place where it says the man with the palsy had faith to come to Jesus. After all, he was bedridden and probably had no hope of ever being different. His four friends had the faith to not only find the house where Jesus was, but when they saw that the crowd kept them from entering through the door, they went up to the roof, broke it up, and let down their friend in his bed. Just think of it! It wasn't even their roof they destroyed! What faith they had! In verse 5 it says Jesus saw <u>their</u> faith, but he said to the one who was sick, "Son thy sins be forgiven thee." This story has an interesting twist to me. The man's friends had faith Jesus would heal their friend of his palsy. Yet, Jesus' first act was to forgive that man's sins. It was not until the end of a monologue about forgiveness of sins directed to the scribes, in the presence of this sick man, that Jesus turned to the man and healed him (verse 11). Even with that healing, we don't see where the palsied man ever had faith for himself. Jesus in His mercy just healed him so God could be glorified.

When someone requests prayer from me personally for a *physical* healing, I don't pray specifically for that unless God tells me to. God may want to heal them in other areas first. Instead I ask God to direct me how to pray. I don't believe this is a lack of faith on my part, but rather during that prayer time I am asking for the gifts of discernment, prophecy, a word of wisdom and/or a word of knowledge.

Another example of a healing based on a family member only is in Mark 5:35-end. A ruler of the synagogue approached Jesus and told him his daughter was dead. Now he sure had faith--more than those who told him in verse 35 to not bother the Master any further. His daughter did not have any faith. How could she? She was dead. Jesus told the ruler to "Be not afraid, only believe" (verse 36). Jesus went to the house, took her by the hand, and she arose. Everyone else was astonished, but not her father. He was the only one with any faith, yet Jesus healed his daughter.

Another example that healing can be by your faith alone is found in Matthew 20:30-34. Two blind men sitting by the wayside, hearing Jesus was passing by, cried out to him for mercy. The multitude rebuked the men since the multitude had no faith, but the two men did not stop crying out. Jesus stopped and asked them what they wanted, and they said, "That our eyes may be opened." We see Jesus had compassion on them and touched their eyes. Immediately they received their sight and followed him, yet no one had faith in this story except the two men.

A similar experience happened when my daughter was 6½ years old. She had been diagnosed with pneumonia, been in the hospital in an oxygen tent for a couple of days and was finally sent home with the usual antibiotics and instructions for bed rest. The doctor told me at the time she would always have scars in her lungs, showing she had pneumonia. However, my daughter had faith Jesus would heal her if we only asked. Frankly, I didn't have that kind of faith, but that evening as I tucked her in, she asked me if both of us could pray for her to be healed. As I sat down on the bed and bent over her, I laid my hands on her chest and prayed for a healing, never really expecting anything dramatic. I did know if I laid hands on her as an act of obedience, God would answer our prayers somehow, but I certainly wasn't ready for what happened next. My hands got very hot, and I knew the Lord was doing something. I had my eyes closed and was simply praying when my daughter said she felt a jiggling inside. She said, "He's here, Mommy," and indicated He was standing behind me. Well, I can tell you I received the fear of the Lord at that moment, because my back immediately began to burn as well. Anyway, I said to her, "Who is here?" (In my heart I knew, but I wanted to be sure she knew.) Very softly she said, "Jesus." You'd better believe I got real serious about praying right then. After what seemed like an eternity, I got brave enough to ask my daughter "What does He look like?" As she described Him, I felt as though everything in my heart was exposed. She said He was in a white garment outlined with a bright, white light and with long, white curly hair, but she couldn't see His feet, because He was kind of floating. She said He had eyes like BBQ coals when they are red hot. Then she said there was something coming out of his mouth like a knife instead of a tongue. I could hardly breathe since I knew we were in the presence of the Lord Jesus. She was describing the same Jesus that John saw in Revelation 1:13-16. (Now remember, she was only 6½, and of course was only beginning to read simple things, let alone read the KJV version of the Bible where Jesus is described this way.) I could not move. Then she asked me, "Mommy, do you want to see Him?" Of course, I was freaking out inside, but didn't want her to know, because He was manifesting Himself to her as the loving, healing Jesus she had asked for. I told her, "No, but we need to keep praying, because He is healing you." For a long time there was silence between us as the heat in my hands and on my back continued to burn. Then the heat dissipated from me, and at the exact moment it did my daughter said, "He's gone." I had faith she had seen a vision, but only she had the faith to be healed. She immediately felt better, but I still had her finish her antibiotics. However, as with all physical healings, the credibility is in the medical records. When we returned to the doctor and he took another x-ray, he said it was amazing, but her lungs showed no signs of her ever having had pneumonia. I considered this to be a miraculous healing, but I really didn't have the faith it took--only my daughter did--and Jesus in His mercy healed her. After her healing, she made a banner portraying the Jesus she saw, and she still has that banner today as a reminder of His goodness to her. Here it is.

Definition of the Manifestational Gifts

      This brings us to another way Jesus heals today. Sometimes it is a sign, with no one really having faith, and the Lord just moves in His mercy. One example in the Bible is Luke 22:50-51. This was right after Judas betrayed Jesus with a kiss, and one of Jesus' disciples cut off the right ear of the servant of the high priest. Jesus simply spoke, "touched his ear, and healed him." No one had faith for a healing--in fact, no one was even asking for a healing. Interesting isn't it? God moves in His own mysterious way.

      A healing following a scriptural principle like this happened to me when I was in my early thirties. I had been taking thyroid pills for about ten years. The doctor had told me that this was a medication I would always have to take, sort of like blood pressure medicine. Once you start the medication, you never go off, so I never gave it a thought that this was something God could heal me of. When I moved to Oregon, I needed to find a new doctor and obtain new prescriptions, but I ran out of my thyroid medication before I could do that. I was busy with my two children while relocating to a new place to live in an unfamiliar state, becoming involved in a new ministry, meeting new friends, etc., and I just never got around to finding a new doctor. It was several months before it dawned upon me that I had not been taking my thyroid medications and had not been having any symptoms I had previously. God in His mercy, once again, moved in a way that I did not expect. I never prayed for a healing, yet I received one. Why? I think one reason is so I could share with those who are dogmatic about God only healing one way.

      Of all the gifts, I have always wanted this gift of healing so I could lay hands on people for dramatic results--for physical, instantaneous, miraculous healings for others, and it's the one gift that I have the least faith for--an <u>immediate</u> physical healing. God hasn't used me in the realm of physical healings that I can remember, except with my daughter. I don't know if God hasn't used me this way because I don't need it, or if He knows I'd get lifted up in pride, but it is one gift I'd really like to have working more in my life.

      Jesus has an attitude of healing towards the world. However, the gifts of healing are given to believers, first to build up His body, and then for healings to be experienced by those in the world as a tool for salvation. Therefore, as the Body of Christ gets strong in the Word, we should be receiving healings, and others should see our lives, bodies, and minds being healed. As this happens, gifts of healing can be linked with evangelism. When these gifts work together, healthy believers produce other healthy believers.

      (Not only is this a **manifestational** gift, it is also a role exercised within the church as a **ministry** gift, and as such, has a different administration. As a role or church office, it would become observable by others that when a specific person prayed for a healing for someone, healings would consistently happen. Please refer to the previous Chart of Categories of Spiritual Gifts on page 16.)

      By now I hope you are seeing that one result of studying and exercising the gifts is that your God will get bigger--not that He was smaller and now He is bigger, but rather, you will begin to see Him with bigger eyes.

Working of Miracles

Definition: The supernatural intervention of God into the normal course of nature as God has established it. It can be a mighty, wonderful, instantaneous work that may include healing; or it can be a supernatural process that is not instantaneous, having nothing to do with a healing, but is above man's expectations and/or abilities.

Many believers and unbelievers experience miracles in their lives. However, the working of miracles is different. It is an operation that occurs when a person exhibiting this gift is <u>used consistently</u> to meet various needs. The outward appearance of working of miracles will vary around that person. They will be a person of prayer, spontaneously asking God to meet a need and then standing back to see how He will accomplish His will in that situation. Mark 10:27(b) says, "... With God all things are possible."

The working of miracles is spoken of (though not specifically described) in Acts 8:5-6. Philip was preaching and the people with one accord gave heed to Philip, "... hearing and seeing the miracles which he did." Also in verse 13 it says, "Then Simon, **(the sorcerer)**... believed also: and when he was baptized, he continued with Philip, and wondered, beholding the miracles and signs which were done."

Acts 20:7-10 tells the story of Paul and Eutychus. While Paul was preaching:

> ... a certain young man named Eutychus, being fallen into a deep sleep... and fell down from the third loft, and was taken up dead. And Paul went down, and fell on him, and embracing [him] said, Trouble not yourselves; for his life is in him. And they brought the young man alive, and were not a little comforted.

Now someone who was raised from the dead--that was certainly a miracle!

Are you familiar with how Corrie ten Boom was released from the concentration camp, Ravensbrook?[1] Years after she was released, she found out that **all women her age** were put to death, not freed. Some said it was a clerical error, a mistake, but God used that clerical error to release her. That was a modern-day miracle! She lived a life of praying for miracles and seeing them happen.[2]

I do not pretend to have this gift, nor do I know anyone personally who does. However, I have had numerous miracles happen to me in everyday life and have known many people who have experienced miracles throughout their lifetime. Since God says this is a **manifestational** gift He has for his children and a **ministry** gift that operates as a role within the church, I believe there are people with this gift today. I have heard about such ministries, but I just haven't had personal experience with anyone in this ministry. Perhaps some day I will.

One miracle that happened to our family I still cannot explain. Well, that's the nature of miracles isn't it? We were living in Monterey and I was not working. We did not have a steady income, but somehow each month all our bills were met. Some months I could look at our income and say, "Yes, we were employed and made enough for bills," but many times I wasn't even sure where the next meal was coming from. At the end of the year, when it came time to file our taxes, our total year's rent alone was more than our entire income. How did that happen? It was a series of small and large financial miracles.

---

[1] Movie *The Hiding Place*, credits at end.
[2] Corrie ten Boom and Jamie Buckingham, *Tramp for the Lord*. Copyright © 1974 by Corrie ten Boom and Jamie Buckingham. All rights reserved.

Another thing that happened to me that I consider a miracle is how an IRS past-due tax bill was paid. Because of our previous financial problems while living in Monterey, we filed our tax returns, but couldn't always pay them, so they gained interest and penalties for three years. We could not see the light at the end of the tunnel, but I believed God would somehow provide before the IRS came and repossessed any of our belongings. We had written letters, negotiated partial payments, and finally the IRS said that within thirty days they would come to take our non-business tools and vehicle to sell if we did not pay the amount owed. There was no way we could borrow what the banks considered too small an amount. We couldn't even borrow from family, so we stayed on our knees in prayer. Then I got a call from the Court in Monterey. I'd had an outstanding judgment for over ten years against a private party that I never expected to collect. It turned out that party was brought before the Court system in another county on a case unrelated to me. That Court discovered the outstanding judgment I had and also discovered that party was in the process of selling a historical house. The Court levied a lien against that escrow, and I unexpectedly received the monies owed on my judgment. As it turned out, there was enough to cover the back taxes, buy my daughter her first car (which we had been praying for and which she desperately needed as a college student), and put some money in a bank account for my son. Talk about an unexpected blessing, and I am no different than you! When we have a need, God will always come through--maybe not the way we expected, or had hoped, or even prayed for, but He will meet our needs.

(Not only is this a **manifestational** gift, it is also a role exercised within the church as a **ministry** gift, and as such, has a different administration. As a role or church office, it would become observable by others that when a specific person prayed for someone or something, a working of a miracle would consistently happen. Please refer to the previous Chart of Categories of Spiritual Gifts on page 16.)

Prophecy/Prophetic Utterances

Definition:
1. *To foretell events, scriptural or otherwise; and/or*
2. *To spontaneously speak under inspiration of the Holy Spirit; and/or*
3. *The ability to so know God's overall purposes that one is able to determine how an event or situation fits into that plan.*

Peter refers to the written prophetic word which includes both the Old and New Testaments in II Peter 1:19-21:

> And so we have the prophetic word confirmed, which you do well to heed as a light that shines in a dark place, until the day dawns and the morning star rises in your hearts; knowing this first, that no prophecy of Scripture is of any private interpretation, for prophecy never came by the will of man, but holy men of God spoke as they were moved by the Holy Spirit.

This is the bottom-line of our scriptural authority. We can add nothing to it, and we should not take anything away from it.

In the verse above, prophecy is defined as "pertaining to a foreteller ('prophetic') of prophecy, of the prophets."[1] At all other times prophecy, prophesied, prophesy, or prophesy(ing) in the New Testament means "prediction (scriptural or other)" and "to foretell events, divine, speak under inspiration, exercise the prophetic office."[2]

This gift is mentioned in all three Biblical lists and within those lists has a three-fold application as shown above.

However, specifically as a **manifestational** gift, I think it exhibits itself as a spontaneous prophetic utterance. Wayne Grudem defines the gift of prophecy as "telling something that God has brought to mind."[3] Fredrick Dale Bruner defines the gift of prophecy as being:

> ... spontaneous and direct spiritual communication... not to be confused with preaching or prepared remarks where the substance is obtained by more conventional or indirect means than immediate inspiration. The Spirit delivers His mind and heart spontaneously and directly to the assembly through His prophets.[4]

This is how I view the spontaneous prophetic utterances I have received and heard from others with this gift.

Certainly throughout Acts, Peter and Paul displayed this gift in this way. Though they both knew the Old Testament and God's nature, they spoke spontaneously from God's heart and mind whatever it was God wanted that particular audience or individual to hear.

This gift is not limited to the apostles or the twelve disciples. Ordinary believers just like you and I receive this gift. In Acts 21:9 we are told Philip had four daughters who prophesied (prophetesses). I have to laugh at God's design of giving four women in the same household such a verbal gift.

As I learned more about the Holy Spirit and how He works, my faith grew, and I began to understand and believe what Jesus says in John 16:13-14, NKJV:

> ... when He, the Spirit of truth, has come, He will guide you into all truth; for He will not speak on His own [authority], but whatever He hears He will speak; and He will tell you things to come. He will glorify Me, for He will take of what is Mine and declare [it] to you. All things that the Father has are Mine. Therefore I said that He will... declare [it] to you.

---

[1] *Strong's Concordance*
[2] *Strong's Concordance*
[3] Wayne Grudem, *Systematic Theology.* Copyright © 1994. All rights reserved, p. 1049
[4] Fredrick Dale Brunner, *A Theology of the Holy Spirit: The Pentecostal Experience and the NT Witness.* Grand Rapids: Eerdmans, 1970, page unknown.

You see, prophecy springs from the motivation in God's heart that He wants to talk to you. He gives you this gift because He knows you intimately and what you will do or even think <u>before</u> you do. He wants to take you into His confidence in things pertaining to you.

This gift has a lot of questions and curiosity surrounding it, especially in non-charismatic churches. There are so many things I could elaborate on, but I want to share about things that I have personally observed or experienced as a lay person in a church.

I want to spend a lot of time on the gift of prophecy, because Paul exhorts us over and over that this is the one gift that edifies (encourages) the church as a whole, more than the others. This gift frequently ties in with the gifts of teaching and exhortation but doesn't necessarily have to. If the words spoken are inspired by God, they won't contradict the Bible.

I Thessalonians 5:20 says, "Despise not prophesyings." Prophecies should be chewed on, mulled over, or thoughtfully considered--like the word "Selah" in the Old Testament that is a musical rest. When reading Psalms and you run across the word "Selah", it is not to be spoken, but rather you are to consider what just preceded it, and think about those words. This is the same way we are to consider prophecies.

This gift needs to be handled very delicately. If something has been revealed to you ahead of time, others may find you very hard to live with. It might seem to them you are always spiritually right. Of course, no one is always correct, which is why we test the gifts. This is why attitude and motive are very important in exercising this gift.

When the Lord speaks to you or you are in a group where a prophecy (prophetic utterance) is delivered, you should write it down accurately (word for word) and date it. When it is fulfilled, record the date of fulfillment and how it was fulfilled to see if it was accurate. This leaves little room for interpreting on your part. Our minds tend to change wording or forget exactly what was said. If you elaborate on its wording, it opens the door for pride, and "I" steps right in with opinions or advice that God may never have intended.

When you receive a prophecy (prophetic utterance) from the Lord, if God is leading you to share it, it takes faith to deliver it. You'll probably feel ill at ease, especially if you are not an outgoing person. If you quench the Spirit, because you're insecure about speaking a prophecy, you may feel physically uncomfortable. At times my stomach may start to have butterflies, and if I do not share it with the person(s) God has shown me to share it with, eventually I may even get a headache.

It is possible to step aside in your human nature and let the Spirit move without your own thoughts and designs getting in the way. It will take some conscious effort on your part, and probably won't be a natural thing at first, but if you ask for the mind of Christ, it will become easier with experience.

I experience prophecy (basically hearing the Lord) in a variety of ways. Sometimes it is an impression cutting across my thought pattern, or it may be a small voice within, or an impression on my heart. It may be a phrase in a song. The song might not even be a Christian song, but its message will still be something God wants me to pay attention to. It could be audible. For me, the gift of prophecy can be words I see with my eyes open or closed, in shorthand, or like a ticker tape. Once the Lord even gave me a prophetic vision in the form of sign language, which I do not know, but the person it was meant for did know sign language. It can be a word, a phrase, or an entire thought at a time. It is something you hear with your spiritual ears or something you see, like a vision.

It has been my experience that if you speak what you hear, or write it down to be judged and shared later, God will probably give you more. You may not know the complete prophecy (prophetic utterance) when you start speaking it. You may have to finish what you hear before He'll give you more. It could be incomplete and come in stages. This reinforces the need for prayer when you receive any gift from the Lord.

One question people ask is, "How is this gift different from the Old Testament prophets and the prophets of today?" Well, first of all, the Old Testament prophets had the Holy Spirit come <u>upon</u> them for prophetic inspiration. They were not <u>indwelt</u> by the Holy Spirit as the New Testament believers are. They were also called by God to the office of prophet, and had to be 100% correct in their predictions or else they were stoned. By God's mercy, that standard is not for today. Aren't you glad?

Spiritual Gifts

The *gifts of the Holy Spirit* have been given to the church since Pentecost, but the *ministry of gifts* is seen throughout the entire Bible. God's gifts, flowing through certain chosen people, were manifested in the Old Testament as the Spirit came and went. By contrast, in the New Testament, once a person is born again, the Spirit comes to supernaturally reside in them and does not come and go.

In the Old Testament, people sought out the false prophets for guidance, because they didn't like what the true prophets were foretelling. They chose to go to false prophets instead of going to the Lord. It is not to be the practice of the believer today to <u>seek</u> a prophecy, because that is fortunetelling. As a believer, we are told not to be involved in witchcraft. I Samuel 15:23, NKJV says, "For rebellion [is as] the sin of witchcraft, and stubbornness [is as] iniquity and idolatry." The New Testament passage in Galatians 5:19-21, NKJV says, "Now the works of the flesh are evident, which are... sorcery **(witchcraft)**... of which I tell you... that those who practice such things will not inherit the kingdom of God."

Instead, as a believer, we are to seek Jesus first. God may then use a Christian prophet to confirm something to you or another believer. This may come in the form of guidance or a new direction. Ideally, a Christian prophet should confirm what God has already told the believer. The prophetic utterance should not be a complete surprise to him or her, but if it is, it should be confirmed through God's Word and by Godly counsel of others. Whenever I receive a prophecy for someone else, I pray that it will not be a bombshell to that person, but rather a confirmation of what the Lord has already told them. Sometimes they need the nudge of the Holy Spirit through a person, because they are not listening to God or are dragging their feet and not obeying.

In the Old Testament there were "false prophets." Today there are also "false prophets," which means there are also false prophecies. The Old Testament tells us of one way to test a prophecy (prophetic utterance). "And if you say in your heart, 'How shall we know the word which the Lord has not spoken?' when a prophet speaks in the name of the Lord, if the thing does not happen or come to pass, that is the thing which the Lord has not spoken; the prophet has spoken it presumptuously; you shall not be afraid of him" (Deuteronomy 18:21-22, NKJV).

The key word here is **presumptuously**. We are not perfect. "We know in part and we prophesy in part" and "... now we see through a glass, darkly" (I Corinthians 13:9 and 12). So we must be willing to consider we may be wrong. We learn and grow when we share what we think we heard from the Lord. If we have an attitude that our prophecies are perfectly heard and spoken, this reflects a presumptuous attitude. Although a prophecy may be false, that does not necessarily mean that the person exercising the gift of prophecy is a false prophet intentionally trying to deceive the hearer. Rather, they may be personally convinced God has spoken to them, but they don't have a submissive heart and are not willing that the words they have spoken should be tested. When you exercise this gift, if it is judged false by others, don't be condemned. Perhaps a prophecy you shared was not done in a spirit of humility, or perhaps the person receiving it is not mature in their understanding of how the gifts work. Don't let Satan condemn you. This is exactly how Satan stifles growth in a believer--through guilt and condemnation. You're just the vessel, and you should consider it a learning experience. Don't take it personally. Don't let this cause you to cease prophesying if that is the gift the Lord has given you. If you prophesied with a true heart you are not what the Bible calls a "false prophet" or a wolf.

A wolf is discerned or exposed when he intentionally prophesies falsely and bears poor or no fruit in his life, so we should always judge the prophecy (prophetic utterance) and not the person. Sometimes we don't like the package a prophecy comes in. Look at the Biblical prophets. Jonah probably smelled horribly and looked pretty scroungy while shouting and walking the streets of Ninevah after living inside a whale. Jeremiah was just a teenager when his ministry began, so he was ignored and probably felt like a failure at times. John the Baptist was a wild man--in looks, how he delivered his message, and the things he ate. If any of those three people prophesied in a church today, their message might be rejected just because of the package it came in.

The scriptures tell us to "judge the prophets" (and what they are saying). The best way to discern the difference between a true Christian prophet and a false prophet is by their fruit. You may ask, "What if we don't know them personally?" One thing I ask myself is, "Are they under church authority?" In other words, are they speaking with the pastor's permission? If they are, how do we know what they are speaking is true? How can we know that on the spot? Again, we go back to testing through the scriptural grid I've already shared under the word of knowledge. A true prophecy will not contradict God's Word or God's nature. To judge a prophecy (prophetic utterance) that someone else gives, you judge whether or not it lines up with scripture and God's nature. Some prophecies can be proven or judged as being from God right then, as it is obvious, but others are futuristic or not as apparent, and you must wait on them to be fulfilled before they can be judged or proven true.

My first experience with a false prophet was in a church I regularly attended, and he was our new pastor of just a couple of weeks. It was Easter Sunday, and the theme of his message was supposed to prepare us for communion. As he talked, he began saying Jesus' blood was not different than ours, that Mary was not a virgin, that the Bible was full of errors, and that we were not born sinners, among other things. I couldn't believe what I was hearing. As I looked around the church I couldn't believe what I was seeing. Everyone seemed mesmerized by his message. His blasphemy was causing me to squirm, yet no one else seemed to be picking up on his lies. I kept thinking, "If what he says is true, why are we even partaking in the Lord's supper?" I could see he was playing church just to keep the people appeased, yet he didn't believe the Bible was true. (Today we call people who believe this way liberals, but in the 1960's, this was not a common term.) Anyway, I began to get physically ill, and actually felt the sensation of nails in my hands and a feeling on my head like the crown of thorns pricking me. Of course, it was not as severe as what Jesus felt, but it was a physical manifestation that made me realize this pastor was a wolf in sheep's clothing. Soon afterwards, as soon as I could get my loose ends tied up with the ministries I was leading, I left that church. I am so glad the Lord gave me discernment of spirits and guided me out.

The next question people usually ask is, "What if a prophet is foretelling a future event?" Again, you listen to what is said and run it through a scriptural grid. Then you prayerfully wait. If it is of God, it will come to pass. Put it out of your mind, on the Holy Spirit shelf. If it is of God, He will confirm it. Ask God to show you these confirmations. You don't have to work at it--let the Holy Spirit show you. You don't want to miss them!

Based on this way to judge a false prophet, the story of Jonah brings many questions to mind. Jonah was a prophet, and God gave him a message to give to the city of Ninevah. He was a man of God, called to do God's will, who initially ran the other way. However, after proclaiming God's will, the city repented, from the King on down, and Ninevah was not immediately destroyed. Ultimately the city was destroyed, but not in Jonah's lifetime. We only know that in the hindsight of history. Under the Old Testament criteria, that a prophet of God was to be 100% correct, one might think Jonah was a false prophet. Prophecy (then and now) is to be judged. Revelation 19:10 says, "… the testimony of Jesus is the spirit of prophecy." We know Jonah was not a false prophet (although it might have appeared so in those times), nor was this a false prophecy, because it was "the mind of Christ, the testimony of Jesus." It did a work in the king's heart first and then the citizens' hearts, and they repented--which is God's ultimate purpose for everyone. I bring up this point because sometimes it may appear that a futuristic prophetic word was not accurate. It is at this time one must wait on the Lord. We may not have perfect understanding as to God's timing in bringing a prophetic word to pass, but that does not mean it was not from God. If it is of God, He will fulfill it. That is God's job, and He's perfectly capable. Just remember the Old Testament prophets spoke about the second coming of Christ where **some** of the message was fulfilled, and **some** is still to be fulfilled. "… one day [is] with the Lord as a thousand years, and a thousand years as one day" (II Peter 3:8).

We must be careful not to set a timeline, interpret, or manipulate a prophecy (prophetic utterance). It is natural to assume that the fulfillment of a prophecy will be right around the corner, but that is not necessarily so. Just as with a word of knowledge or a word of wisdom, when I receive a prophecy, I immediately write it down, word-for-word, if possible, because our minds have a way of changing or forgetting the exact words if we don't. Then I date it, and when fulfilled, record the date of fulfillment and how it was fulfilled. This leaves little room for interpreting it your way, and will give you immense joy, ultimately increasing your faith when you see just how the Lord brought it to pass.

A person I believe was a modern-day prophet, though now deceased, was Dr. Francis Schaeffer. He called our nation to wake up to the sliding path we were (and are) on--in particular he warned of the domino effect of humanism, abortion, and euthanasia. He foretold the direction we were headed as a nation, and the ramifications of not standing in the gap with prayer decades before others recognized what was going on in these areas. He was proven correct.

We really shouldn't be astounded to find this gift so readily distributed by God and used in the church today. After all, Paul said in I Corinthians 14:1 and 5 that his desire was that <u>all</u> believers in the Corinthian church would prophesy, so we can have great confidence to come boldly before the throne of grace and ask God for this gift.

The first time I received the gift of prophecy it was as though a ticker tape was going across my spiritual eyes--word-for-word. I thought to myself "What is that?" but as I spoke each word, another one came. I had to step out in faith and speak each word before God would give me the next word.

As I grew in exercising the word of wisdom, the word of knowledge, and prophecy individually, the Lord began giving me two or three gifts at the same time. Remember how I said the gifts grow and develop in stages in a person's life? Well, God in His graciousness would give me words first for myself and as I obeyed them, or believed them in faith, He began giving me words for others. As I shared them, most of the people were receptive--but not always. As I learned to step out in faith sharing these words with the person I believed they were for, I noticed that sometimes they would not acknowledge that it made any sense to them right then. This was a real stretch of faith for me just to share--and to not have it acknowledged was even harder. It was always a real lesson in humility and caused me to go back to God for His confirmations. However, as I would see these words come to pass in their lives, I began to realize that often people cannot acknowledge the truth you have just spoken when God pierces their hearts. It may be denial, blindness from the enemy, fear, or embarrassment. After all, when you don't really understand that God's love includes correction at times, it can really take you by surprise to realize that He has revealed something only you know about yourself to someone else for the express purpose of bringing it to light. Once it is in the light, the enemy has no more power over you in that area. It is then up to you to walk in that light. "For you were once darkness, but now [you are] light in the Lord. Walk as children of light" (Ephesians 5:8, NKJV).

If one is not walking in love, I think this gift lends itself <u>most readily</u> to pride. After all, when one gives a prophetic word, one is representing that God Himself is behind that utterance for that person at that time. It is a very heavy responsibility to bring God's Word or words to bear on a person or situation. One must walk humbly and meekly.

Recently, I was worshipping in church, and the Lord surprised me with a scripture. I immediately ran it through my Biblical grid of testing that I mentioned earlier.

1. Is this scriptural? It was a scripture so that was a cinch to figure out, but I wanted to make sure I didn't apply it out of context.
2. Does this apply to me? Upon reflection, it was a scripture the Lord had given me personally about twenty years prior. Therefore, I asked:
3. Does it apply to someone else? Immediately the Lord gave me the person's name. I did not know this man's circumstance, so I asked what I was to do with it. I got no answer, so I did what I always do in those cases--I put it on my Holy Spirit shelf.

A few months later, I began teaching a class on the **motivational** spiritual gifts and this man attended. I remembered the prophecy, but God did not release me to share it with him. At the end of the class, eight weeks later, when I presented an evaluation of his particular **motivational** spiritual gift, I also shared that scripture with him regarding a trial he had been going through for a long time. His wife who was present said, "Do you remember that was the same scripture I gave you last night?" Talk about a confirmation! It was in God's perfect timing--not mine. If I had spoken too soon, back when I first received it, it would not have had the impact that it did then. Well, that wasn't the end of the story. About a month later, this man went to a conference a couple of states away. No one knew him there, but he was prayed over, and a prophecy came forth. Guess what it was? Yep! The same scripture his wife and I had given him a few weeks earlier. Do you think the Lord is driving a point home with him? I do. I'm sharing this so God will get the credit--not me, nor his wife, nor the people who prayed over him. It's all for the purpose of building up this man in particular and the Body of Christ in general so God will be glorified.

Occasionally I will receive a prophecy for someone else that disturbs me. It will seem negative. That is when I pray against it, that it would not be fulfilled. The principle for praying that a prophecy would not occur can be found in Acts 8:18-24, NKJV. After Simon the sorcerer saw Peter and John lay hands on people and they received the Holy Spirit, he wanted to buy the Holy Spirit's power. Peter rebuked him and said, "Repent therefore of this your wickedness, and pray God if perhaps the thought of your heart may be forgiven you." Then Simon said, "Pray to the Lord for me, that none of the things which you have spoken may come upon me." So, you never know if your prayer will change the course of that prophecy being fulfilled.

Prophecies help us in day-to-day decisions, so as God speaks to you for others, ask for the faith to share the prophecies with those involved.

(Not only is this a **manifestational** gift, it is also a role exercised within the church as a **ministry** gift, as well as a **motivational** gift within individuals. Please refer to the previous Chart of Categories of Spiritual Gifts on page 16.)

If you want a more thorough explanation about the gift of prophecy from those operating within the national and international church arenas, I'd recommend *Developing your Prophetic Gifting* by Graham Cooke, *Thus Saith the Lord?* by John Bevere, or *Surprised by the Voice of God* by Jack Deere. Again, I'm addressing these gifts from my own circle of influence, as a lay person's perspective.

Discerning or Discernment of Spirits

Definition:
1. *A judicial estimation as to whether or not God is in a situation, such as spiritual gifts, words, actions, attitudes;*
and/or
2. *A supernatural sense causing one to be aware of a person who is:*
   a. *opposed to Christ or*
   b. *possessed by a demonic being or*
   c. *an evil influence*

This gift is not "discernment" but "discernment of spirit<u>s</u>", (plural). This includes both good and evil spirits as well as the superhuman, such as an angel, demon, or God.

Discerning of spirits is only referred to two times in the Bible--I Corinthians 12:10(b) and Hebrews 5:12-14.

Points 2a, b, and c include, but are not limited to, cults and the occult.

The first time I realized that there really is a spiritual war going on for souls, was when I was baptized in the Holy Spirit. The Lord opened my eyes to a heavenly realm where I saw Satan's demons fighting against God's angels for a decision I was about to make to either accept or reject the "baptism of the Holy Spirit." This was my first experience with the gift of discerning of spirits in a heavenly realm. Since then, I have known without a doubt that Satan and his evil angels are just as real as God and His angels are.

The story in Acts 13:6-11, NKJV of Paul, Barnabus, and Bar-Jesus (or Elymas the sorcerer) is fascinating to me.

> Now when they had gone through the island to Paphos, they found a certain sorcerer, a false prophet, a Jew whose name was Bar-Jesus, who was with the proconsul, Sergius Paulus, an intelligent man. This man called for Barnabas and Saul and sought to hear the Word of God. But Elymas, the sorcerer (for so his name is translated), withstood them, seeking to turn the proconsul away from the faith. Then Saul, who also [is called] Paul, filled with the Holy Spirit, looked intently at him and said, 'O full of all deceit and all fraud, [you] son of the devil, you enemy of all righteousness, will you not cease perverting the straight ways of the Lord? And now, indeed, the hand of the Lord [is] upon you, and you shall be blind, not seeing the sun for a time'. and immediately a dark mist fell on him, and he went around seeking someone to lead him by the hand. Then the proconsul believed, when he saw what had been done, being astonished at the teaching of the Lord.

Paul was able to discern that this sorcerer's purpose was to keep the proconsul from hearing God's Word. After Paul exposed him and his practices, the proconsul believed. What an evangelistic tool this gift can be!

In my early thirties, I met a man on an airplane. He seemed like a nice guy, very friendly and personable, as we talked about neutral things. Then he said he "perceived" we had passed over the border from California to Oregon. When he said that, my spiritual antennas immediately zoomed in, and the Lord started to minister to me to tell him about Jesus. I started questioning him about spiritual matters, and he shared he was into Eckanakar and their beliefs. I knew Eckanakar was, and is, a cult.[1] He was real mellow and spacey as he talked. But as I began to share with him about Jesus, he started to get edgy and wiggled about in his seat. The Lord told me I had a captive audience and to press the matter of the Gospel, so I did. But, the more I shared, the more physically distressed he became. When the pilot announced we were landing in Eugene, but to remain seated with the seat belt fastened, he became so unglued that he jumped up and began ransacking the racks above us, throwing the bags around trying to get to his. The stewardess warned him to sit down, and he started making noises under his breath. He was in such a hurry and so desperate to get out, that as soon as the plane stopped, he pushed her aside even before the door was open. I'm sure he was being influenced by a demon in some way. No one had to tell me about this gift of discerning of spirits in other people--I just knew.

Discerning of spirits as defined in Point 1 above is a gift, which I think, is much needed in the administrative/leadership role in the church today. Even though it is a spiritual gift, we must learn to exercise it (Hebrews 5:12-14). Woe to the pastor or elders who do not have a "judicial estimation as to whether or not God is in a situation, such as spiritual gifts, words, actions, or attitudes."

I was in a church once where the pastor had the gift of discerning of spirits, but his elders' board did not. He had inherited this board from the previous pastor, and in many instances his decisions were questioned, because they could not spiritually see the situation. He told me the Lord had shown him that as new elders were considered to serve, that discernment of spirits was one gift he would look for.

In Matthew 16:21-23, Jesus had just finished describing to his disciples how he must suffer in Jerusalem, be killed and be raised again the third day. Peter jumped in saying, "Be it far from thee, Lord: this shall not be unto thee." Then Jesus said to Peter, "Get thee behind me Satan...." This shows us how Satan influenced Peter's mental disposition and caused him to be opposed toward Christ at that point in time.

Probably the best scriptural example of being possessed by a demon is in Mark 5:1-9 where Jesus spoke past the man living among the tombs to the indwelling spirits and cast them into the swine. We looked at this story under gifts of healing, but it has a double gift application. In both instances, notice Jesus was in control. Just remember, He always is. I John 4:4 says, "... greater is he that is in you, than he that is in the world." James 2:19 says, "... the devils also believe, and tremble." Both of these scriptures are very comforting to me. I hope they are to you too. There is no need to fear Satan if the Holy Spirit dwells in you.

---

[1] Source: Ekanakar is a Religion of Light and Sound, with an office in Canyon Lake. Copyright © 2000–2005 ECKANKAR. All rights reserved. Last modified June 8, 2005   050503 (Lake Elsinore, California). Online posting as of 3/10/05. http://www.eckankar.org/siteMap.html

One time I was part of a prayer team asked to a woman's home for specific healing prayer. She had some small children, and she asked her teenager to watch them while we prayed. As we began to focus on her healing, loud noises came from the adjoining walls—thumping, bumping, and pounding. It was quite a distraction, and I changed my focus from praying about her to asking the Lord to quiet the children. I thought they were so rowdy. I couldn't understand why her husband, who was also praying with us, didn't go see what the problem was and calm them down, as the teenager in charge was obviously not in charge. After about fifteen minutes, I opened my eyes to see if anyone else was as distracted as I was. It seemed no one else was being disturbed. They were all privately praying or taking turns offering prayers. It was at that point that I decided to ask God what was going on. He revealed to me that Satan was trying to keep me from hearing God's voice in this matter, so (in my mind) I concentrated even more on praying for a healing. The Lord began to reveal to all of us at once the source of this woman's sickness. It seemed we had turned a corner prayer-wise, and she began to confirm that what we were hearing from the Lord was true. When we left, one of the other women on the prayer team approached me and said, "Did you hear those kids acting wild in the other room?" I was amazed she had also heard them and told her that at first they kept me from hearing from God. Then we asked the rest of the team if the children bothered them at all, and no one else knew what we were talking about. No one else had heard the noises. That was when we both realized the noise was not the children but instead, spirits trying to hinder our prayers, and only the two of us were given the gift of discerning of spirits for that situation.

I believe this is the hardest gift to stand firm on and exercise in faith. Because this gift is not tangible in the natural realm, others may not see what is so clear and obvious to you in the spiritual realm. When you have the gift of discerning of spirits, you just know.

In the story in Acts 16:16-18, the young girl was saying all the right things, but was disruptive to Paul as he taught. It took Paul awhile (in fact many days) to catch on to the fact that he was dealing with a demon-possessed girl. Once he did, he rebuked her, and the evil spirit left her. This is a combination of Points 1 and 2 above.

When I quench this gift, I find discerning of spirits frequently gives me a physically uncomfortable feeling in the depths of my very being without having any facts to back it up. Often when God starts manifesting this gift in you, you will have very little to go on except feelings. You will often feel an inner turmoil and not know why. You must go back to the Word, and test your feelings against what God says.

In addition to the above, there are lots of false doctrines surrounding this gift in Christian circles. One that is particularly distressing to me is attributing all depression or insanity to evil spirits. Sometimes depression could be purely physical, such as a chemical imbalance within the brain. Another doctrine that rears its head about this teaching is whether or not a Christian can be possessed. The following two scriptures indicate to me why I do not believe Christians can be possessed in their spirit, if the Holy Spirit is living in them. "Can two or three walk together, unless they are agreed" (Amos 3:3, NKJV)? "For you are the temple of the living God" (II Corinthians 6:15-16(a), NKJV). Sometimes a conversation with a person will reveal the difference between whether they are depressed, oppressed, or possessed.

This gift includes discerning both good and evil spirits as well as if there's no spirit involved. By that I mean, sometimes a person is not sick due to a spirit. It is a sickness that is not due to any specific spiritual condition but is a sickness as a result of the general fall of mankind. Jesus talked about this in John 9:2-3 when his disciples asked him why this man was blind. "Master who did sin, this man, or his parents, that he was born blind." Jesus answered, "Neither... but that the works of God should be made manifest in him." There was no overt sin that caused his blindness. A modern example might be arthritis. It is a degenerative disease that is probably a direct result of the fall and is not necessarily the result of a specific sin in a person's life. I hope you see how discernment of spirits is a very useful gift especially when encountering confusing situations whether praying for someone else or yourself.

Various Tongues

Definition: A God-created language exercised by the speaker that has not been acquired naturally, studied, or learned.

Romans 8:26, NKJV says: "Likewise the Spirit also helps in our weaknesses. For we do not know what we should pray for as we ought, but the Spirit Himself makes intercession for us with groanings which cannot be uttered." Sometimes these groanings are our emotions deep within crying out with sounds that we cannot express in words and may not be a prayer language at all. I believe this passage also refers to times in prayer where we may simply run out of words in our native language. It is at this time when the Spirit helps us exercise a private, yet personal prayer language which is not in our own native language. This prayer language is one application of the gift of tongues.

When I have been praying by myself for the same thing over a long period of time without apparent results, or maybe I've had a prayer request for which I have asked others to pray, eventually everyone involved may run out of ways to phrase the request. Perhaps I just simply run out of words or ideas altogether. I might not be able to figure out a new prayer game plan. In fact, if a prayer is not being answered, people need to ask God why. He may reveal a different way to approach it. That is where the gift of tongues may come in.

There are many studied approaches to the different types of tongues--*private*, *public*, and *sign* tongues. I Corinthians 14 deal with both *private* and *public* tongues and Acts 2 is considered by some to be a *sign* tongue.

Rather than go into a detailed teaching on these different approaches, in keeping with the reason for writing this letter initially, I want to share my own personal experiences instead. There is so much mystery and misunderstanding about this gift that perhaps my practical approach will help you become more comfortable with this gift, whether or not you ever use it.

More often than not when people mention the topic of spiritual gifts, the first thing they think of is tongues, and they plant themselves right there, not wanting to know the truth about this gift. Sometimes this even stops them from wanting to learn about or experiencing the rest of the spiritual gifts. How sad this is to me, because I have counted approximately twenty-seven gifts that are not the gift of tongues. You are robbing yourself of so many blessings if an abuse of tongues is keeping you from experiencing any of the other gifts.

Admittedly, there have been abuses of tongues in many instances. Instead of asking, "Where is God in all of this?" one immediately writes off tongues as not having anything to do with God. Without further study, or asking the Lord Himself, they decide it is something they don't want. Sometimes the confusion occurs with someone who has had no experience with this gift, or confusion happens with the visitor to the church, not necessarily the regular church attendee. If this has been your experience, I can certainly understand your reaction. Remember I came from a main-line, non-charismatic denomination, so when I see what appears to me to be emotionalism in a church service that I personally am uneasy about, the first thing I ask myself is, "Is there confusion?" If so, I know Satan is in there somehow stirring up the pot. "For God is not the author of confusion but of peace..." (I Corinthians 14:33). The second thing I ask myself is, "What is the fruit of this person the rest of the week, not just on Sunday?" Whether I know the person(s) or not, that helps me settle down. God will minister to me if it is from Him or not, and as I focus on Jesus, I have learned not to be distracted by what might be going on around me.

Each time I have done a Bible study on the word tongues in Acts, it has helped me see all the different ways God worked, so as not to be dogmatic about the way this gift is exercised. Being rigid about this gift is what I have noticed leads to abuses.

I Corinthians 13:1 tells us there are at least two types of tongues--"tongues of *men* and tongues of *angels*." It seems logical to me that "tongues of *men*" are languages spoken on earth, yet unknown as the native language to the speaker. When I read about angels in the Bible, I read that angels praise God. Psalms 148:2 says, "Praise ye him, all his angels: praise ye him, all his hosts." Therefore, I believe "tongues of *angels*" is the heavenly language of praise, not known to anyone except angels and God (unless it is interpreted).

In Acts 2:1-11, those speaking in tongues were understood by those from different countries, because the tongues were heard by each individual in their native language. These tongues were for the purpose of conversion as well as a general witness to the crowds. Perhaps this is what Paul meant when he referred to "tongues of *men*."

I Corinthians 14:2 and 14 says that those who speak in an unknown tongue speak to God. It is the Holy Spirit within you, as a believer, who is speaking to God. This gift bypasses the intellect, which is why even though you do not know what you are saying, your spirit will be lifted. Whether tongues are spoken privately or publicly, they will be praise, petitions, or intercession for someone.

When I was initially introduced to hearing tongues spoken by others, I was curious, and when I heard singing in tongues, I thought it very beautiful. Paul talks about singing in the Spirit (tongues) in I Corinthians 14:15. I believe when we sing in the Spirit in tongues, we are singing "tongues of *angels*." Of course we can sing in the Spirit in our native language as well.

The following references could also be references to singing in tongues. Ephesians 5:19 refers to "speaking to yourselves in... **spiritual songs**, singing and making melody in your heart to the Lord" and Colossians 3:16 says, "... admonishing one another in... **spiritual songs**, singing with grace in your hearts to the Lord."

In the late 1960's, when I was curious about the gift of tongues, I visited a lot of Christian groups. Occasionally I would find myself in groups where I felt pressured to pray for this gift for myself. When I did not receive it right there on the spot, I felt like less of a Christian because of the attitude of those around me. I hope this never happens to you. However, if it does and if you are teachable, you have an opportunity to learn and grow from it. As a result of feeling pressured, for about three years after I received the baptism of the Holy Spirit, I refused to ask God for this gift. I wanted all the others, to be sure, but not this one. Then one day God spoke to me and said, "Why do you despise one of my gifts?" I answered Him and said, "Who me?" As we continued our conversation, He told me I despised the gift of tongues because of what I had encountered myself or observed in others. I felt like I'd had cold water thrown in my face. I immediately determined I would ask for that gift privately, and if God chose to give it to me, I would accept it.

Then one day when I woke up I heard a voice deep inside me speaking in another language. The best way I can explain it is that it sounded like my stomach was gurgling, but it was in syllables. As I listened, I knew it was the Holy Spirit interceding on my behalf. As I began to repeat those words which sounded like syllables to me, I was overcome with such joy that I understood what it meant in I Corinthians 14:4 where it says tongues edifies the person speaking. It sure does, and do you know why? You are <u>immediately in the throne room</u>.

Not long afterwards I heard that another believer in our church received this gift while singing in the shower. I thought that sounded pretty safe, and since I am musically inclined, I thought I'd like to receive it that way. Of course, God has His own way of dealing with each of us on a personal level, and I did not receive it in the shower. Instead, one day much later, at home I began to sing a hymn, and I became aware of another set of words in my head going along with the tune. As I began singing those words, I began to sing in tongues. I was pleasantly surprised, and I had such joy I didn't want to stop singing. One neat way to get started is to start singing a familiar melody you know. I personally like a familiar melody from an old hymn, and then I start praising the Lord in tongues. Doing this immediately takes my mind off my surroundings and circumstances, and I'm able to concentrate on Jesus, which frees me up to worship Him in a different way.

Did you know you can stop and start speaking or singing in tongues at your will? I didn't know that initially. In I Corinthians 14:18-32, Paul talks about exercising certain vocal gifts publicly. His instructions indicate they can be spoken out loud or not--at your will. An individual is not overtaken by something they cannot control when speaking in tongues or prophesying.

Even the types of tongues are given at God's direction. Some people have both types of tongues. I have at times spoken in another earthly language (*men's* tongues) and at other times spoken in a heavenly language (*angel's* tongues). In a public setting, tongues of either type are a divine miracle for the benefit of the listener. It doesn't make a difference as far as the speaker is concerned. But since I am often curious as to which kind I am speaking, I wanted to include some comments about them. When I first began speaking in tongues, I would ask the Lord if I was speaking another language (*men's* tongues) or if I was praising God (*angel's* tongues), and often He would let me distinguish between the two even if I didn't get an interpretation. Either *men's* or *angel's* tongues can be interpreted by the person speaking or by another person present. However, I have now learned over the years that when I'm speaking in tongues I can tell the difference by the sounds of the syllables. I can also tell if I am praising God or interceding as the tone of the tongues will change. I have simply learned these things through experience and confirmation by others.

Tongues are a very practical gift. Sometimes if you are requested to pray for someone, you don't have a lot of time to focus on God's characteristics or have time to spend in worship and praise. Sometimes there is a need to pray immediately, but the setting is not conducive to meditative prayer. Or, if you don't know what to pray, you can pray in tongues. Romans 8:26 says we can know by faith that the Holy Spirit knows what to pray and is praying things we don't know anything about but that are in God's perfect will. It can be either *men's* tongues (an unknown earthly language to you) or *angel's* tongues.

I Corinthians 14:2 tells me that when I pray in tongues, the Holy Spirit within me is giving me utterances which are from me to God without an intellectual understanding on my part or anyone else's part. It is an unknown language to me at that moment. Any interpretation given to the speaker or to another person is revealed to the person's spirit, not their intellect. If used privately, it builds up one's spirit. If used publicly with an interpretation, it builds up the church. The gift of interpretation of tongues is the next gift we will discuss.

Of course, when a tongue is interpreted, it also has to be judged the same way a prophecy or a word of knowledge is judged as we have discussed previously. With the gift of tongues, the main thing to keep in mind is to do things "decently and in order" (I Corinthians 14:40).

I was in a public church meeting once where tongues were spoken spontaneously, and it was not part of that church's order of worship. The pastor immediately stepped in and encouraged the church to wait for the Lord to speak an interpretation. It was very comforting to be a part of that church, because I felt protected spiritually.

(Not only is this a **manifestational** gift operating within individuals, this gift is also exercised as a **ministry** gift or role within the church, typically as a prayer or prophetic ministry. Please refer to the previous Chart of Categories of Spiritual Gifts on page 16.)

In I Corinthians 14:13 we are told that if you have this gift, you are to pray for another one-- interpretation of tongues. Some people believe that each person can only have one gift. If that were true, why would God tell us to ask for this pair of gifts? This is the only gift with specific instructions to pray for an accompanying gift, so let's look at the other half of the pair.

Interpretation of Tongues

*Definition: The supernatural ability to explain the utterance of tongues thoroughly--either yours or someone else's. This is **not** a translation, as in a word-for-word rendition, but rather a general trend of thought or message.*

I Corinthians 14:2-5, NLT says:

For if your gift is the ability to speak in tongues, you will be talking to God but not to people, since they won't be able to understand you. You will be speaking by the power of the Spirit, but it will all be mysterious. But one who prophesies is helping others grow in the Lord, encouraging and comforting them. A person who speaks in tongues is strengthened personally in the Lord, but one who speaks a word of prophecy strengthens the entire church. I wish you all had the gift of speaking in tongues, but even more I wish you were all able to prophesy. For prophecy is a greater and more useful gift than speaking in tongues, unless someone interprets what you are saying so that the whole church can get some good out of it.

When I was first becoming familiar with the orderly operation of tongues in prayer meetings, I came across a time when someone spoke in a tongue, but there was no immediate interpretation. I had a general trend of thought, but did not speak out, because I did not realize it was the interpretation. How did I know? At that exact moment I didn't, but in God's graciousness, as there was a pause in the prayer, another person spoke the same thought I had, although not word-for-word. Therefore, I could judge it as being the interpretation to the tongues spoken, and it was confirmed later when we discussed what had transpired in the meeting.

It is important to wait for an interpretation. If a tongue is given in a meeting, wait on the Lord to give the Spirit a chance to move. The Spirit is quenched if a tongue is given and before any interpretation can be given, someone else speaks a prophecy or another prayer request. Of course, you can't wait forever for an interpretation, but it is up to the leader of the group to linger for a few moments before moving forward with the meeting.

At another prayer meeting, as I was praying, the Lord told me if I would speak the tongues He gave me, He would give the interpretation to another person in the room, and He named that person. Well, let me tell you it was real risky on my part, because I didn't know if that person had either the gifts of tongues or interpretation. However, I did obey. I spoke out in faith, and she received an interpretation and a prophecy, not knowing the Lord had previously revealed this to me. This was very encouraging to both of us, because then we knew without a doubt God was operating in union with our prayers.

I have been in meetings where tongues are spoken with a message in a native tongue immediately following. This could be the interpretation of the tongues, or it could be a prophecy, or both could be spoken. Many times there is confusion as to thinking <u>any</u> utterance following a tongue is the interpretation. An interpretation of the tongues would be praise or intercession, because **it is the Holy Spirit in a believer speaking to God.** If the message following the tongues is in the form of instruction or exhortation, then I believe it is a prophecy not an interpretation, because **it is words from God to the believer.** Do you see the difference? Paul talks about this in I Corinthians 14:2-4. The gift of tongues is the Holy Spirit inside of us talking to God. The gift of prophecy is God talking to us.

Sometimes there are several prophecies, sometimes totally unrelated, following one utterance of tongues. This may cause uncertainty among those listening that does not glorify God. In my experience, the interpretation will sound different in tone and actual words than a prophecy. Often the way an interpretation can be judged is, two people get the same interpretation, and the Lord reveals it to them simultaneously.

Discovering your Manifestational Gifts

By now, I hope you're starting to recognize that the **manifestational** gifts do not seem to operate independently, and often there is an overlap. It may be hard to distinguish where one ends and the other begins, such as with a word of wisdom, a word of knowledge and/or prophecy. It takes some degree of faith to exercise any of the gifts. Sometimes it may be the **fruit** of faith and sometimes the **gift** of faith, but I don't worry about that too much. I just bask in His glory and the fact that God has chosen to let me in on another piece of His work at a given time in my life.

We see in Acts 15:32 that Judas and Silas were not apostles. Yet, they not only exhorted the believers (gift of exhortation), but they also were prophets. This is another example that the spiritual gifts are for the ordinary Christian just like you and me.

Do I believe all the gifts are for today? I sure do. I believe the Bible teaches that, and my life testifies of it too.

I also hope you are continuing to recognize by all my scripture references, I lean heavily on the Word first and the gifts second. To turn those around is to ask for problems. We must be growing in the Word to recognize His gifts when they are exhibited.

I have discovered that God does not give His gifts if you are not going to use them for His kingdom, but He will give them beyond your wildest imaginations if you are open to moving with the Holy Spirit. The **manifestational** gifts become more evident when I am praying for, with, or about someone or a situation. He does not expect perfection, but He does give you the faith and require obedience when He opens your spiritual eyes to His gifts. As Billy Graham has said, "Although His limitless resources are available to us, He will permit us to have only as much power as He knows we will use or need...."[1] "The Spirit-filled life is not abnormal; it is the normal Christian life."[2]

---

[1] Billy Graham, *The Holy Spirit*. Copyright © 1978. All rights reserved, page 156.
[2] Billy Graham, *The Holy Spirit*, page 157.

CHAPTER 9

Definition of the Miscellaneous Manifestational Gifts
I Corinthians 7:7 and Matthew 19:12

Manifestational Gifts: Special manifestations that take place in and through a believer, according to need, by the working of the Holy Spirit.

Singleness/Celibacy (Eunuch)

Definition: Being single or unmarried and celibate for the Lord.

According to Jesus in Matthew 19:12, NKJV:

All cannot accept this saying, but only [those] to whom it has been given: For there are eunuchs who were born thus from [their] mother's womb, and there are eunuchs who were made eunuchs by men, and there are eunuchs who have made themselves eunuchs for the kingdom of heaven's sake. He who is able to accept [it], let him accept [it].

The word "gift" mentioned in I Corinthians 7:7, where Paul is speaking about being single, is the same word "gift(s)" mentioned in I Corinthians 12:1 and Romans 1:11 which refers to "spiritual gifts." It is called "charisma" and means "a spiritual endowment."[1] Therefore, many theologians conclude that being single for the Lord is a spiritual gift.

When Paul elaborates on this gift in I Corinthians 7:7, he is speaking out of his life's experiences detailed in Acts 5, 6, 8 and 9. If we follow the story, we may be able to understand why many commentators think Paul probably had the gift of being single at the time he wrote I Corinthians. We know Gamaliel was a Pharisee (Acts 5:34) and was on the Sanhedrin Council. Paul, previously known as Saul, was also a Pharisee. Paul tells us he studied under Gamaliel, so he probably was on the Sanhedrin Council too. Acts 8:1 says Saul approved (consented) to Stephen's death, which meant he was voting in favor of it. Commentators tell us that to cast a vote on the Sanhedrin Council one had to have been a male Jew, married at the time, or a male Jew who had been married in the past. Therefore, this is Paul's authority to speak as one unmarried on the gift of being single, yet also able to minister to the married couples in I Corinthians 7:7.

The following three ways are examples how the gift of being a eunuch[2] might occur:

1. Born a eunuch.
2. Castrated. Most references in the Bible to eunuchs refer to state officers called chamberlains. They were men who were castrated so they could be employed in or appointed to positions of guarding the Oriental bedchambers, generally for a King. The first chapter of the book of Esther has just such an example. However, some references to eunuch in the Bible refer to employees of the governors who were not castrated.
3. Your choice to serve God for a time or season as a single person (a eunuch "for the kingdom of heaven's sake.")

Many people choose to remain single by their own willpower for a specific time period, usually while they complete a goal. However, I'm convinced, if you ask in faith, as a believer in Jesus Christ, you can receive the spiritual gift of being single (a eunuch) which can make this decision much easier to fulfill. This gift is not something you decide to do on your own strength. God can and will give this gift if your circumstances warrant it. It is easier to serve God when you are single. There are fewer distractions in ministry, and your vision is not as easily hindered since you don't need to consult a spouse about your choices. Some examples of the gift of being single could be as a single parent or a single missionary.

---

[1] *Strong's Concordance*
[2] A man or boy whose testicles have been removed or do not function. Encarta Dictionary: English (North America)

Spiritual Gifts

After my first marriage I had two children to raise alone. I wanted to focus on them and on serving the Lord without distractions. As I observed other single parents struggle with the dating game and relationships, I realized those things did not interest me. I just wanted to serve Jesus. This gift lasted for five years. I never asked for this gift, but instead, somewhere along the line, I realized that it had been given to me. I believe this was a fulfillment in my life of Point 3 above.

If you receive this gift, you will discover peace, joy, and contentment with being single. You will not be hindered by a sexual tension that many singles combat. You won't be looking at every cute guy or girl and wondering, "Is this the one for me?" Your passion for Jesus will outweigh any passion for the opposite sex during this season in your life.

I know of a pastor who asked for this gift while in seminary. He was able to study God's Word without being concerned about meeting a potential wife and becoming distracted in his priorities. After he graduated, the Lord lifted the gift from him, and his eyes were opened to his wife-to-be. Guess what? She had been in the same seminary all along, but he was unaware of her since he had a single vision that did not include developing a relationship with the opposite sex until he graduated. The Lord honored that goal by giving him the gift of being single for a specific time.

Dreams

Definition: Something seen in sleep as a visual enhancement to scripture or a situation.

It seems to me there is a tendency for dreams and visions to be more misunderstood and misinterpreted more than the other gifts.

In Numbers 12:6 God is speaking: "And he said, 'Hear now my words: If there be a prophet among you, [I] the Lord will make myself known unto him in a vision, [and] will speak unto him in a dream.'"

Acts 2:17 is a quote from Joel 2:28 as a promise for New Testament Christians. "And it shall come to pass in the last days, saith God, I will pour out of my Spirit upon all flesh: and your sons and your daughters shall prophesy, and your young men shall see visions, and your old men shall dream dreams." Since this passage speaks of sons and daughters, young and old men, in the context of "all flesh," I do not think it limits dreams only to old men, nor does it limit visions to young men or any of the other gifts to certain groups or individuals. Once again I try not to limit God. I have had scriptural dreams, and in every church I have been in close community with, I have known people who have had scriptural dreams too.

However, the Old Testament does speak more of dreams than the New Testament. Therefore, we need to keep a balanced view regarding this gift. I'm not skeptical of Christians receiving dreams, but I am prayerful about their source. Basically, all references to dreams in the Hebrew and Greek in both the Old and New Testaments have the same meaning.

Genesis 41:32 says, "And for that the dream was doubled unto Pharaoh twice; [it is] because the thing [is] established by God, and God will shortly bring it to pass." Sometimes I have dreams that repeat themselves, don't you? Well, after I read this, I realized that maybe God was trying to get through to me, and I wasn't paying attention to Him the first time, so if I dream something more than once, I pay special attention to its content.

There are three sources of dreams, and we should ask for discernment as to their source.

1. Jeremiah 23:26-27 and verse 32; 27:9-10; and Zechariah 10:2 tell us about the first source-- Satan using false prophets.
2. Ecclesiastes 5:3(a) tells us the second source could be "the multitude of business" which often comes out in dreams as we sleep. If we are worrying about something or even just thinking about it as we go to sleep, we may wind up dreaming about it.
3. The third source is described in Joel 2:28 and Acts 2:17. It is the best kind of dream since it is from God. Two familiar examples of dreams from God are in Matthew 1:20 where Joseph dreamed about Mary's pregnancy and Matthew 2:12 where the wise men were warned in a dream of Herod's plot to kill Jesus.

According to Madame Jeanne Marie Guyon,[1] there are several purposes of dreams.

Doubtless you will wonder that I, who makes so little account of things extraordinary, relate dreams. I do it for two reasons; first out of fidelity, having promised to omit nothing of what should come to my mind; secondly, because it is the method God makes use of to communicate Himself to faithful souls, to give them foretokens of things to come, which concern them. Thus mysterious dreams are found in many places of the Holy Scriptures. They have singular properties, as

To leave a certainty that they are mysterious, and will have their effect in their season.
To be hardly ever effaced out of the memory, though one forgets all others.
To redouble the certainty of their truth every time one thinks of them.
They generally leave a certain unction, a divine sense or savor at one's waking.

---

[1] Madame Jeanne Marie Guyon (1648-1717 a.d.) *Madame Guyon* (autobiography) Moody Press, Interlibrary Loan, S.F. Public Library, Class No. BG993, Acc. No. 72-43, pg. 202

Another purpose is to cause the person to seek the Giver more intensely in prayer. It also should cause the person, even an unbeliever, to seek God instead of astrologers or fortunetellers. Sometimes dreams given to an unbeliever will put the fear of the Lord in them. In Daniel 2, you will notice that Nebuchadnezzer was an unbeliever.

As a rule, dreams just happen as you're minding your own business sleeping. (By that I mean, I don't ask for God to give me guidance through a dream, I just ask for guidance, and sometimes it comes later in the form of a dream.)

Dreams usually are instructional for a specific situation rather than ongoing for daily guidance. Sometimes a dream gives visual enhancement to a scriptural passage or a situation. But always remember, the Word is inerrant, constant, and clear and is to be used for guidance on a daily basis.

The best way to properly recognize the source of a dream in your own life, or that of someone else's, is to ask for the gift of discerning of spirits. God will tell you when it's from Him and confirm it through His Word. Sometimes symbolism is present, so you may need to ask for an interpretation (which is also a gift). Don't try to figure it out, and don't be in a rush to receive an interpretation. Often an interpretation will come much later, not necessarily the minute you wake up.

I don't regularly dream, so when I dream and remember it, I'm pretty confident God is letting me know something specific. I usually don't remember my dreams until the Lord recalls them. I write them down, date them, and set them aside on my Holy Spirit shelf until the Lord brings them back to mind. Then I either mark down when and how they were fulfilled or just jot down what God seems to be telling me as an interpretation for future reference.

I would venture to say that most dreams are the multitude of our daily business. The gift of discerning of spirits will reveal from which source the dream is coming.

For me, a dream from Satan is unusually disturbing and may also bring feelings of terror or fear with it. A dream from God may also disturb me momentarily, because of my lack of understanding, but upon waking, there is no torment accompanying it.

God may use your name personally when He speaks like He did when He spoke to Moses, Samuel, Paul, and Cornelius, just to name a few. When you first recognize His voice, it may seem to come out of the blue, but He's been talking to you long before that. "How precious also are Your thoughts to me, O God! How great is the sum of them! [If] I should count them, they would be more in number than the sand..." (Psalms 139:17-18(a)). His thoughts towards you have been constant and without number long before you became aware of Him. As you respond and spend more time with Him, you'll hear Him more frequently, and you will not be taken aback by His voice as often. It will surprise you every time, but it will not be a shock that He would actually speak.

One time I was preparing a teaching on dreams for a Bible Study, and I had a dream about foot washing. Since I wasn't particularly interested in the subject of foot washing at the time, rather than praying about it, I dismissed the dream as being a multitude of my daily business. Then a few days later I heard a Bible study about Jesus washing the disciples' feet. Suddenly I remembered my dream and realized that it was meant to be a personal lesson to me. God showed me principles about foot washing that I later developed into a Bible study. He also showed me the practical application of God-given dreams through that dream.

Genesis 37:5-10 gives us an account of two dreams Joseph had from God, as well as two interpretations which his brothers and father interpreted. Interpretation of dreams is the next gift we will discuss.

Interpretation of Dreams

Definition: a God-given insight, understanding, or solution for understanding or to open up dreams for yourself or others.

Genesis 40:5-23 gives us an account of the same dream given to two different men. God gave the interpretation to a third person who did not have the dream. Guess who? Joseph. In verse 8 Joseph says, "Do not interpretations belong to God?" Therefore, we see it is God who interprets a dream--not us. We must be careful not to attach our own understanding to a dream from God. I have observed this is the most common mistake one makes. We are just so excited about a dream--we excitedly wonder, "What could it possibly mean?" This causes us to jump to premature conclusions. We need to pray for an interpretation. God will confirm any interpretation through scripture or another means. We must learn to be patient until He does that and not "lean to our own understanding."

In Genesis 20:3-7 God came to Abimilech and warned him (even though he was an unbeliever), not to touch Sara. Abraham had lied to him, saying she was his sister, but God in his mercy revealed this to Abimilech. He not only had a dream from God but it was as clear as day to him what he must not do. God gave him an interpretation, so there would be no misunderstanding, and Abimilech obeyed. God had a plan and did not want Abimilech innocently interfering, so some dreams and interpretations are for protection.

In Daniel 2 there is an account of Nebuchadnezzar dreaming and Daniel interpreting that dream and giving God glory in verse 20.

Recently I asked God to show me how the spiritual gifts can be used to defeat Satan. I had a dream whose details faded with time, but the principles remained strong in my mind. It was a dream that gave me the answer I was seeking. Upon awakening, as I pondered over the dream's symbolism, scriptures accompanied it for an interpretation. Often, when asking for guidance in my life, God may send the answer in a dream. He may do the same for you if you are spiritually alert that this is another way God guides us.

Jeremiah 23:28, NKJV says, "'The prophet who has a dream, let him tell a dream; and he who has My word, let him speak My word faithfully. What [is] the chaff to the wheat?' says the Lord." This principle applies to the dream I shared earlier about foot washing that God put in my mind as I slept, (which was like a temporary piece of chaff) so when God gave me a scripture (wheat) as an interpretation, I would be especially attentive to what He wanted me to know.

Daniel 1:17 tells us "Daniel had understanding in all visions and dreams." Daniel 7 describes a succession of dreams and visions. After seeking the Lord in verse 16, God gave him the interpretation.

Visions and their interpretations are the next two gifts we will discuss.

Visions

Definition: An ability to view an appearance, whether real or mental, to discern clearly, to perceive.

Sometimes the difference between visions and dreams are hard to discern. Job 33:14-16, NKJV says, "For God may speak in one way, or in another, [yet man] does not perceive it. In a dream, in a vision of the night, when deep sleep falls upon men, while slumbering on their beds, then He opens the ears of men, and seals their instruction." This "vision of the night" which Job describes was a "revelation, especially by a dream."[1] When God is trying to get through to you and can't, because your days are filled with your own thoughts and activities, sometimes He uses the time when you're sleeping to speak.

The same principles apply to visions as to dreams regarding their purposes, sources, and how to interpret them. Unless it is very clear that I am awake or asleep, I don't spend a lot of time trying to figure out which it was--a dream or a vision. If I am confused, I just let the Lord tell me if He wants to. Whichever it is, I ask for an interpretation. I also ask for a scripture to go with the vision. The scripture at least sheds some light on it. Often it is the complete interpretation.

In the New Testament, visions are different from dreams, and more often than not, you can tell the difference by reading the surrounding story. In the Old Testament it is sometimes hard to distinguish between them. Both should be judged by God's Word using the scriptural grid. Visions are given according to your measure of faith, just like all the gifts.

We already looked at Numbers 12:6 where I emphasized dreams, but if you re-read it, you will see God also emphasized visions. "And he said, 'Hear now my words: If there be a prophet among you, [I] the Lord will make myself known unto him in a vision, [and] will speak unto him in a dream.'"

Proverbs 29:18 says, "Where [there] is no vision the people perish." Visions are also defined as spiritual imagination. This is another way the gift of visions exhibits itself. This is a different kind of vision. A visionary person is typically a leader with spiritual imagination. Often this gift is given to a pastor to keep his flock from becoming lukewarm. Since the early 1970's, I am thankful that the churches where I have been actively involved, have been on the cutting edge of Christianity, with pastors exhibiting a pioneering spirit.

I had a friend who was also an elder with the **motivational** gift of leadership, who owned some property with a home on it that was not used regularly by his family. The house was within a comfortable driving distance from our church, yet remote enough to make you feel you were out of civilization. The Lord gave him the vision or spiritual imagination to let the church use that property for small group retreats or family getaways. It was a wonderful blessing for our church to have a secluded place that cost nothing for an overnight escape from our every-day schedules.

Because I am not very creative visually or artistically, when I spiritually see something, I am pretty sure I am not imagining it. I am usually confident that God has revealed something to me. One time the Lord gave me a vision in sign language. The person I was praying with knew sign language, but I didn't know she did, so I simply described what I saw. God also spoke a prophetic word in an unknown tongue to me. When I shared the vision, she knew immediately what it meant. Later the Lord gave the interpretation of the prophetic word to both of us. As you can see, God is the creative one, not me. This is another beautiful way the Body of Christ works together.

Now I want to share the variety of ways visions can be experienced. Ann Graham Lotz describes the way she sees images as in her "mind's eye."[2] Often I hear of Christians who get pictures or images in their mind's eye but are unaware that they are having visions.

Visions come in so many ways. Perhaps you have already had a vision or two but didn't know that was what it was. Once you know it is just another way God speaks to His children, you will look forward to God interpreting them to you.

---

[1] *Strong's Concordance*
[2] Ann Graham Lotz, *Angel Ministries*, Fall 2005 Newsletter

Examples of ways <u>visions</u> come to me are:
1. Out of the blue (a surprise). Actually all visions come out of the blue, unexpectedly, and are a surprise to our flesh.
2. During formal, intentional prayer, usually with my eyes closed.
3. Open eyes
4. Color
5. Black and white
6. Still
7. Moving
8. Awake (as opposed to dreams while I'm asleep)

All of these examples and more can be seen in scripture too.
1. Out of the blue—a surprise
2. During formal, intentional prayer--Cornelius (Acts 10:30)
3. Open eyes--Elisha's servant (II Kings 6:15-17)
4. Color--Daniel (Daniel 7:7-16)
5. Black and white--Isaiah and many minor prophets received the Word of the Lord by a vision. If they did not describe them in color, I think they may have been in black and white. (Isaiah 1:1)
6. Still--Saul/Paul (Acts 9:3-9)
7. Moving--King Belshazzar. Notice that this King was an unbeliever. God is not limited in the way He works to witness to someone. (Daniel 5:5-end)
8. Awake—Peter, as if in a trance. (Acts 10:10)

Sometimes visions are accompanied by voices or words such as what happened to Abraham in Genesis 15:1.

False visions are described in Jeremiah 23:16, NKJV. "Thus says the LORD of hosts: 'Do not listen to the words of the prophets who prophesy to you. They make you worthless; They speak a vision of their own heart, not from the mouth of the LORD.'" Ezekiel 13:7, NKJV says, "Have you not seen a futile vision, and have you not spoken false divination? You say, 'The Lord says,' but I have not spoken." This is another reminder that we do have to be careful when we receive a supernatural message in some form or other.

Interpretation of Visions

Definition: The ability to know by faith what a vision means, either yours or another person's.

In Daniel 5:5 to the end, King Belshazzar saw a vision of handwriting on the wall and didn't know what it meant, but Daniel interpreted it.

In Acts 10:1-33, a vision was given to Cornelius, but at another time a vision and its interpretation was given to Peter. All this is to show that God is not limited in how He exhibits His gifts to us. We just need to be open to receiving them.

Discovering your Miscellaneous Manifestational Gifts

Again, these **manifestational** gifts will become more evident to you when praying for, with, or about someone or a situation.

Remember we are to have a "warmth of feeling for"[1] the best gifts. If your motive is to glorify God by operating these gifts in love and you make yourself available to other's needs, then God will give you the best gifts at the right time.

---

[1] *Strong's Concordance*

SECTION 3

MOTIVATIONAL GIFTS

CHAPTER 10

Definition of the Motivational Gifts
Romans 12:6-8

Motivational Gift: The gift that drives and motivates you and becomes your spiritual passion.

If you would like to discover your **motivational** gift, I will share some practical tools with you. Most people find it very interesting to go through this process even if they think they already know what their gift(s) might be. I have discovered that many people find these tools confirm their gift(s) and help them feel more comfortable using them.

After you have identified your **motivational** gift, I would encourage you to confirm it to yourself and others by stepping out in faith and exercising it in some kind of a ministry. It may be a ministry in a church or an organization resembling or similar to a church, called a para-church organization. You will begin exercising it as the Lord leads, stepping out in faith, perhaps tentatively, but this is okay.

If you have been given the **motivational** gift of service, an example of how this might express itself is by assisting a pastor or teacher in practical matters so they can be more effective in their ministry.

Or let's say your **motivational** gift is exhortation. You might begin by encouraging (exhorting) others in your church, either one-on-one, or in a group setting about God's methods, promises, and character.

Regardless of which gift you might think you have, ask the Lord for spiritual eyes to see and spiritual ears to hear. You will begin to spiritually see things happening around you that you were not aware of previously. You will also begin to hear people say good things about you. This is called affirmation. *Affirmation is not flattery or compliments. Affirmation occurs when your brothers and sisters in Christ see you through the eyes of God--recognizing how He is working in your life with Jesus as the pattern.* If you give God the glory when you are affirmed, He will begin to add other gifts and ministries to you. You may also receive affirmation for the **fruit** people see in your life or your talents and abilities. Just take the affirmation you receive for any of these gifts, fruit, or talents, and give God the credit (glory) for doing this work in you. You should also be sensitive to opportunities to affirm others as you see God using them. This is how the Body of Christ is built up.

As you grow in your **motivational** gift and are faithful to what the Lord gives you, it may develop into a **ministry** gift recognized by an official title. A **ministry** gift is a role or position within the church. Some churches have ministry titles or departments that fit the lists in Ephesians 4 of **apostles, prophets, evangelists, pastors/teachers**, and in I Corinthians 12:28-30 of **miracles, healings, helps, governments (administration), and tongues**. Some churches do not recognize all these gifts as official roles by title within their church. Regardless, we should remember that it is God who distributes the gifts as He sees fit, not as we think it should be. For example, some churches consider the **ministry** gift of pastor/teacher as one gift. It really doesn't matter to God if you use your gift in an official capacity or not, because He recognizes how, when, and where you are involved in ministering to others. You should make it your priority to walk before God first, with or without recognition by man.

Ministry simply means serving. Over the years I have observed that ministry is a natural thing that happens as God raises you up to be used in your personal circle of influence. Each of us has different circles we travel in that are unique to us that no one else can reach. This is your ministry field, your sphere of service.

Here is one example of how your gift might develop from a **motivational** gift into a **ministry** gift. Let's say, first you discover your **motivational** gift found in Romans is that of teaching. As you study God's Word, you begin to share that Biblical knowledge with people around you, perhaps in an informal setting or one-on-one. Their positive responses might inspire you to talk to your pastor about starting a Bible study, and then you would start developing your gift as a teacher under the category of **ministry** gifts. In this example, your **motivational** gift would be teaching, and your **ministry** gift would be as a teacher. Do you see how this might work? This may be another reason we see an overlap of some gifts in the three lists. You might want to review those overlapping gifts on the previous Chart of Categories of Spiritual Gifts on page 16 before reading the more detailed explanations that follow.

Prophecy, prophets, and prophetic utterances are considered **motivational, ministry, and manifestational** gifts. Teaching and teacher are considered **motivational and ministry** gifts--whereas pastor/teacher is considered by some scholars to be a joint gift and is referred to as a **ministry** gift in Ephesians.

Both service and helps are very similar. In Romans 12, service is listed as a **motivational** gift. Helps means "to aid"[1] and is mentioned only one time where it is considered a **ministry** gift in I Corinthians 12:28 (specifically in KJV).

The gift of governments is also mentioned only one time as a gift in I Corinthians 12:28 (specifically in KJV). Some translations use administration. It is a **ministry** gift.

The gift of ruling is listed as a **motivational** gift in Romans 12:8 (specifically in KJV). Some translations use leadership.

Both governments and ruling are very similar, because they organize people and/or paperwork, but they operate in different ways (I Corinthians 12:5 and 6).

Although these specific gifts are found in more than one list, I believe it is because there are different types of administration and ways of operating. However, it is the same God who gives and distributes them according to I Corinthians 12:4-6. The *same gift* might work *differently* in the *same person* from time to time, or the *same gift* might work in *two separate ways* between *two different individuals*. You cannot predict God's actions or put Him in a box.

I can promise you though, that after you discover your primary **motivational** gift, you will want to move out in a ministry that you are perfectly suited for. This will give you such joy. If you ask for power in your ministry to be used for God's purposes, not your own, the **manifestational** gifts will start to exhibit themselves. Mark 16:17 says, "And these signs shall follow them that believe; In my name shall they cast out devils; they shall speak with new tongues."

I knew a man who had the **motivational** gift of service. He felt called to a short-term mission trip but had no idea what he could do. (Service-gifted people like to do.) He connected up with a ministry group that was strictly evangelistic in nature. They went from door-to-door (or rather village-to-village) and simply shared Jesus. He went in the capacity or role of the **ministry** gift of evangelist. One day as they were sharing the Gospel with a group of people, there was a woman on the fringe of the group who was loud, rowdy, and disruptive. As he and the team began to pray, the Lord revealed to him that she was demon-possessed. This was the **manifestational** gift of discerning of spirits being exhibited. The Holy Spirit showed them how to pray and what they were really up against. There was a need; God found a willing servant, and the woman was freed. God was glorified, and the believers were built up in their faith as a result. However, it was not just the believers who witnessed this situation who were encouraged--anyone who hears about this story grows in faith too. Do you see how this man had several gifts operating, because he was obedient to God's leading?

Now I'm going to put on my teacher's hat and define each specific **motivational** gift, noting its *Characteristics* as well as its *Considerations*. These *Characteristics and Considerations* are not etched in black and white nor written in stone, but seem to make sense through what I have experienced, researched, and heard from other Bible teachers.

In all of us, when our strengths go too far, they become weaknesses. We see this in our temperaments. It is the same with the gifts. When you begin to operate in your gifts, the tendency to react in your human tendencies is always there. The following *Considerations* reflect strengths going too far and you should be aware of them when exercising each gift.

---

[1] *Strong's Concordance*

Motivational Gift: Prophecy

A Biblical character exhibiting this gift might possibly be Peter--Acts 2:14 and 37-40.

Definition: A strong motivation to call people to conform to God's standards.

Romans 12:6 tells us this gift is exercised "According to the proportion of our faith."

One Scripturally motivating verse is Revelation 19:10: "... for the testimony of Jesus is the spirit of prophecy."

Characteristics when this gift is exercised are:

1. Scripturally perceptive (I Corinthians 6--Paul). This person has a unique ability to discern and analyze Biblical matters. They tend to run problems and situations through a Biblical/scriptural grid first.
2. Biblically discerning (Acts 5:1-11--Peter). They can put their finger on the heart of the problem (usually without hours of counseling). These are bottom line people and seem to be able to discern people's hearts, motives, and character, not just their actions or words.
3. Spiritually compelled (Acts 2:14--Peter). They are pushed internally by the Holy Spirit to speak.
4. Bold in the Spirit (Acts 2:38--Peter). Often their approach is painfully direct. When they speak, their words hit you between the eyes with truth. They primarily see things in black and white/right and wrong.
5. Persevering (I Corinthians 5--Paul). They are not satisfied until a Biblical change is made.

Considerations to be aware of:

1. Can appear to be negative and/or critical.
2. Can appear to be arrogant (because there is no compromise).
3. Can appear to be insensitive.
4. Can tend to be intolerant. Almost everyone I have known that has this gift know they need to work on mercy! They need to ask for more of the **fruits** of mercy, which are long-suffering, patience, and self-control, to name only a few.
5. Can tend to oversimplify.
6. Can appear to lack submissiveness to those in authority.
7. May have a lone ranger attitude.
8. Can have a narrow perspective. I believe this may be the hardest gift to exercise properly, because it easily and subtly produces pride and bitterness more than any other gift. It is the gift that is most likely to cause division if not exercised properly.

Scriptures To Balance These Considerations:

"Finally, brethren, whatsoever things are true, whatsoever things [are] honest, whatsoever things [are] just, whatsoever things [are] pure, whatsoever things [are] lovely, whatsoever things [are] of good report; if [there be] any virtue, and if [there be] any praise, think on these things" (Philippians 4:8).

"For I say, through the grace given unto me, to every man that is among you, not to think [of himself] more highly than he ought to think; but to think soberly, according as God hath dealt to every man the measure of faith" (Romans 12:3).

"But speaking the truth in love, may grow up into him in all things, which is the head, [even] Christ" (Ephesians 4:15).

Motivational Gift: Service

A Biblical character exhibiting this gift might be Timothy--Philippians 2:19-23 or Phoebe--Romans 16:1-2.

Definition: The ability to see practical needs within the Body of Christ and the Spirit-led motivation to meet them.

One Scripturally motivating verse is Ephesians 6:6-7: "Not with eye service, as men-pleasers, but as the servants of Christ, doing the will of God from the heart; with goodwill doing service, as to the Lord and not to men."

In Romans 12:7, KJV this gift is called ministry. Ministry is simply serving, and all Christians should serve to the best of their ability. However, this gift of service/ministry is a distinctive type of serving.

Characteristics when this gift is exercised are:

1. Super sensitive to practical needs. They see practical/physical needs in a unique way.
2. Responds quickly to meet needs. Red tape and committees drive them crazy.
3. Task oriented.
4. Finds joy in meeting needs (Philippians 2:20). For them, they do not serve by considering it a labor of love--they just love serving.
5. Has unusual stamina. When serving in their ministry they are very focused--can work hours at a time.
6. Does not draw attention to themselves or their task. They don't necessarily speak about being a Christian--they just live it.

Considerations to be aware of:

1. May appear to be less spiritual than others because they are not as visible or outspoken as other personality types or the other gifts.
2. May have difficulty in saying "No." This may interfere with what God wants to do in other people's lives. They must learn to set boundaries so as not to be taken advantage of and to allow others to respond to a need.
3. May react negatively to a lack of service by others.
4. May have difficulty letting others serve them.
5. May be robbing others of the blessing of serving because they frequently can perform the task better and faster.
6. Can be an enabler if they respond too quickly to a need.
7. Needs affirmation from others because they can easily be taken for granted. This affirmation is not out of a need to be noticed or ego, but because they need to know they're accomplishing something for God.

Scriptures To Balance These Considerations:

A perfect example is the martyr attitude exhibited in Martha's attitude towards Mary in Luke 10:38-42.

Motivational Gift: Teaching

A Biblical character exhibiting this gift might be Luke--Luke 1:1-4.

Definition: The motivation and ability to search out, clarify, and present Biblical truth in a systematic and thorough manner.

One Scripturally motivating verse is James 3:1, NLT: "Dear brothers and sisters, not many of you should become teachers in the church, for we who teach will be judged by God with greater strictness."

Characteristics when this gift is exercised are:

1. Enjoys studying and researching the Bible (Luke 1:1-4). I often consider them a scholar of the Word. They are self-motivated to study the Word. I have personally observed they teach even when they have nothing prepared formally because it's already in their storehouse of knowledge.
2. Very sensitive to accuracy of information regarding God's Word. They are like a detective. They dissect words and meanings.
3. Slow to accept new teaching without checking source.
4. Biblically very exact. For example: Did Adam eat an apple, or did Adam eat the "fruit"? Was Jonah swallowed by a whale, or was Jonah swallowed by a "great fish"?
5. Desires to understand and report on scriptural passages and/or words thoroughly and in much detail. They will study the Word on their own thoroughly enough to teach it whether or not that is their goal.
6. Desires to present Biblical information in a systematic sequence. I have observed that many people with the gift of teaching prefer to study and impart their knowledge in a verse-by-verse, logical account, rather than topical.

Considerations to be aware of:

1. Presentations may be boring/ methodical. Having this gift does not automatically mean one is an effective communicator.
2. May neglect practical application in presentations because they are cognitive oriented.
3. May reduce learning to empirical factual knowledge.
4. May appear to be arrogant due to degree of knowledge. They're a walking library. This can be a real ego booster.
5. May rely more on knowledge or information than on inspiration. They need to ask the Lord for illumination and not just rely on reason or understanding.
6. May be overly critical in spotting factual errors in other's teachings.
7. May have tendency to throw out the baby with the bath water if some fact is not exactly accurate.

Scriptures To Balance These Considerations:

"Knowledge puffs up, but love edifies" (I Corinthians 8:1(b), NKJV).

"And my speech and my preaching [was] not with enticing words of man's wisdom, but in demonstration of the Spirit and of power" (I Corinthians 2:4).

Motivational Gift: Exhortation

A Biblical character exhibiting this gift might be Barnabus--Acts 9:26-27 and 15:36-39.

Definition: The motivation and ability to challenge and encourage others to pursue a Godly course of action.

One Scripturally motivating verse is Hebrews 3:13: "But exhort one another daily, while it is called today; lest any of you be hardened through the deceitfulness of sin."

Characteristics when this gift is exercised are:

1. Sees personal tribulation as an opportunity for growth (II Corinthians 2:9). An Exhorter comes alongside like the Holy Spirit. In my personal observations I have noticed they are often outgoing, constantly affirming, encouraging, and uplifting. They see situations as the cup is half-full as opposed to half-empty. This comes very naturally to them, as they view a problem.
2. Able to visualize Godly, spiritual achievement for others and motivate them to Godly action. They are more than a cheerleader type of person, or an inspiring or motivational speaker, but instead they motivate by Godly principles.
3. Desires personal involvement in helping others deal with life's challenges. They are people-oriented like Barnabus in Acts 9:26-27 or like Barnabus and Mark in Acts 15:36-39.
4. Desires to give precise steps of action in urging people forward in their Christian walk.
5. Desires to make Biblical truth practical and applicable to everyday life (James 1:22). Their greatest concern is how to make the truth work out in life's situations.

Considerations to be aware of:

1. May appear to oversimplify because often their timeframe may be unrealistic--or steps may be omitted in action plan.
2. May appear to be insensitive to the feelings of those being counseled, because they are more achievement-oriented than empathetic.
3. May be accused of taking Scripture out of context, because their enthusiasm for action may take priority instead of Word taking priority.
4. May unintentionally neglect theology or Biblical doctrine in an effort to get someone moving towards a goal.
5. May err on the side of enthusiasm for a non-Biblical game plan instead of spiritual counsel.
6. May overestimate their ability to help others in time, money, and treasures, because of their action approach.
7. Are not necessarily detail-oriented. They may use a scattergun approach when counseling or solving a problem.

Scriptures To Balance These Considerations:

"Be diligent to present yourself approved to God, a worker who does not need to be ashamed, rightly dividing the word of truth" (II Timothy 2:15, NKJV).

Motivational Gift: Giving

Biblical examples exhibiting this gift might possibly be:

1. Church in Corinth--II Corinthians 9
2. Church at Philippi--Philippians 4:14-18

Definition: A strong motivation and ability to contribute material resources to meet the needs of others and to further the work of Christ.

One Scripturally motivating verse is Philippians 4:15, NLT: "As you know, you Philippians were the only ones who gave me financial help when I brought you the Good News... No other church did this."

Characteristics when this gift is exercised are:

1. Loves to give both money and material things to Christians and/or ministries "with simplicity." (Romans 12:8)
2. Views money more objectively than others (Acts 20:35). They operate out of a pure motive with singleness of heart.
3. Understands uniquely that they are earning money to give away first, not earning money to only meet their wants and needs, which is always second. Asks: "How much can I give away?" not "How much do I have to give?"
4. Has an intensified grasp of the eternal investment of money (Luke 12:13-21). They see themselves as channels, not reservoirs.
5. Desires to give quietly. They have no desire for public recognition--prefers anonymity.
6. Has a motivation to practice personal frugality simply as a vessel, not as a result of lack of resources. They may have lots of money, but intentionally look for ways for it to flow through them.
7. May live a simple lifestyle either by choice or limited income. This gift is not exclusive to wealthy people. They look for ways to give money and things away. They hold material items loosely.
8. Has an uncanny ability to see financial needs that others might overlook. They supernaturally see these financial or material needs.

Considerations to be aware of:

1. May appear to be miserly to others.
2. May be impatient with others who struggle with giving, especially if the person with this gift is not walking in the Spirit.
3. May appear less spiritual to others, because it is a gift that operates behind the scenes and others don't see your checkbook.
4. May at times lack wisdom in their giving. Remember--don't let need drive you; let discernment guide you.

Scriptures To Balance These Considerations:

"If any of you lacks wisdom, let him ask of God, who gives to all liberally and without reproach, and it will be given to him" (James 1:5, NKJV).

Motivational Gift: Leadership
(Ruling, KJV)

Biblical character exhibiting this gift might be: Paul--I Corinthians 1:1

Definition: The motivation and ability to lead and organize people and tasks to accomplish the work of the ministry.

One Scripturally motivating verse is Hebrews 13:17, NLT: [regarding spiritual leaders] "... Their work is to watch over your souls, and they know they are accountable to God."

Characteristics when this gift is exercised are:

1. Visionary (Paul--Acts 20:17-end regarding spiritual goals.)
2. Can spiritually envision what could take place and can share it in such a way that others want to get on board.
3. Administrative regarding ministerial matters (Paul--Book of Philemon). They are detailed (even in concepts), are organized, and can delegate.
4. Inspirational (Paul--Book of Philippians). People-oriented. They can turn a Godly vision into reality by challenging people.
5. Tough-skinned (Paul--II Corinthians 11:23-28).
6. Determined/self-starter.

Considerations to be aware of:

1. May appear unwilling to be personally involved because of the ability to delegate.
2. May appear callous to criticism. Nobody likes criticism, but they are so focused and convinced of God's direction, they can withstand more criticism, letting it run off their back like water off a duck.
3. May appear to be over-controlling. Once they have delegated a task, they need to make sure they do not become micromanagers.
4. If there's a leadership vacuum, they'll fill it. Others may think they are always in charge or always doing it their way.
5. May be too competitive.
6. May appear to use people. A leader's objective and priority may seem more important that people's feelings.
7. May be over-demanding with others. Often may be considered a slave driver.

Scriptures To Balance These Considerations:

"Humble yourselves in the sight of the Lord and He shall lift you up" (James 4:10).

Motivational Gift: Mercy

A Biblical character exhibiting this gift might possibly be Epaphroditus--Philippians 2:25-30.

Definition: The unique ability to empathize with and minister to people who are hurting.

One scripturally motivating verse is James 3:17: "But the wisdom that is from above is first pure, then peaceable, gentle [and] easy to be entreated, full of mercy and good fruits, without partiality, and without hypocrisy."

Characteristics when this gift is exercised are:

1. Sensitive. They seem to possess suffering antennas for others' physical, emotional, or psychological pain.
2. Keen awareness when others are hurting. Others who are hurting are attracted to those with the gift of mercy.
3. Empathetic (not just sympathetic). They can physically feel the hurt and carry it home with them.
4. Compassionate. Most people see a need, but don't necessarily know what to say or do. Mercy people naturally and instinctively know what to say or do. This warmth is readily apparent in a church more than any of the other gifts, especially to visitors.
5. Patient. These are long-haul Christians. They are able to maintain a long-term commitment through the crisis.

Considerations to be aware of:

1. May tend to lack firmness when necessary. They need to learn how to set boundaries and take breaks.
2. May be indecisive or lack conviction when instead love needs to be tough.
3. May try to remove hurt instead of letting hurt do its work, because they don't want to cause more hurt. They must remember that God uses pain to develop character.
4. May tend to be overly guided by emotions. Most people are guided more by emotions than God's Word. People with gift of mercy can let emotions drive them, so much so, that it becomes unhealthy for them and the situation. This needs to be balanced with wisdom and discernment.
5. May tend to over commit, because there are a lot of hurting people who can't set their own boundaries.
6. Can't easily say "No." Again, they must learn to set boundaries.

Scriptures To Balance These Considerations:

"... those who by reason of use have their senses exercised to discern both good and evil" (Hebrews 5:14(b)).

CHAPTER 11

Motivational Gift Survey

I have researched and taken many surveys myself, and I have never found one that includes all of the **motivational, ministry, and manifestational** gifts together. By the same token, most surveys include questions that lump gifts, talents, abilities, and even temperament all together. By not separating the questions regarding abilities, talents, and temperament from spiritual gifts, the results do not give accurate indications of simply the spiritual gifts. For that reason, I have included a survey intended to include only the **motivational** gifts in Romans 12.

I've also discovered that once you have a correct evaluation as to your primary **motivational** spiritual gift, you will want to try it out. God wants to move you into a **ministry** so you can glorify Him and "[that] your joy might be full" (John 15:11). Once you are involved more intimately with the Body of Christ, you will see the **manifestational** gifts become a normal, although supernatural, part of your life.

By now I hope your curiosity is peaked and that you've looked at the **motivational** gifts in the previous chapter. Before you settle on which gift you think is yours, let's have some fun and take a survey. These questions are compiled from various surveys, and are not perfect, but they will measure where your giftedness might lie. It is a tool to assess what really motivates you spiritually.

INSTRUCTIONS

Use the next page as your scoring sheet. Then turn to the following questions. You might find it easier to make a separate copy of the scoring sheet so you can easily move it from page to page as you read the questions. Be sure to record your answers by going down the columns, not across.

Read each numbered statement in this survey and ask yourself, "How often is this statement true of me?" Do not spend a lot of time analyzing these questions. If you are stumped, answer as to your SPIRITUAL PASSION.

Please choose one of the numbers below, and then record the answer that best fits each statement about you on the Motivational Spiritual Gift Survey.

3 - If this is <u>always or almost always</u> true about you

1 - If this is true about you <u>sometimes</u>

0 - If this is true about you <u>rarely to never</u>

(I realize this is a weird scoring scheme (3-1-0) but it is correct.)

This is a self-evaluation inventory and there are no right or wrong answers.
Answer as honestly as you can about your own feelings and desires, not what others might see in you.

MOTIVATIONAL SPIRITUAL GIFTS SURVEY SCORING SHEET							ROW TOTAL	TOTAL FOR BOTH ROWS
1._____	15._____	29._____	43._____	57._____	71._____	85._____	_____	} _____
2._____	16._____	30._____	44._____	58._____	72._____	86._____	_____	
3._____	17._____	31._____	45._____	59._____	73._____	87._____	_____	} _____
4._____	18._____	32._____	46._____	60._____	74._____	88._____	_____	
5._____	19._____	33._____	47._____	61._____	75._____	89._____	_____	} _____
6._____	20._____	34._____	48._____	62._____	76._____	90._____	_____	
7._____	21._____	35._____	49._____	63._____	77._____	91._____	_____	} _____
8._____	22._____	36._____	50._____	64._____	78._____	92._____	_____	
9._____	23._____	37._____	51._____	65._____	79._____	93._____	_____	} _____
10._____	24._____	38._____	52._____	66._____	80._____	94._____	_____	
11._____	25._____	39._____	53._____	67._____	81._____	95._____	_____	} _____
12._____	26._____	40._____	54._____	68._____	82._____	96._____	_____	
13._____	27._____	41._____	55._____	69._____	83._____	97._____	_____	} _____
14._____	28._____	42._____	56._____	70._____	84._____	98._____	_____	

MOTIVATIONAL SPIRITUAL GIFTS SURVEY

1. When reading or studying Scripture, I recognize current situations where sin or false thinking has crept in compelling me to share this insight with others.

2. I am drawn to discern deeper or hidden motives instead of taking what people say at face value.

3. I take pleasure in meeting the practical needs of others so they can better focus on their ministries.

4. When I help out in the Body of Christ, I need to know it is appreciated, although I don't care about receiving public credit.

5. I enjoy clarifying difficult Biblical concepts for others.

6. As a student of scripture committed to the learning process, I hope others respect my knowledgeable presentation.

7. The role of guide/advisor is something I desire to be in the lives of those who want to grow spiritually.

8. When someone is struggling spiritually, I am honored when they come to me for guidance, as I believe I can help them.

9. It disturbs me deeply when others don't distinguish the difference between their *needs* and *wants*, as this is crucial to good resource stewardship.

10. My desire to help others when needs arise in the Body of Christ is a major reason I budget my money wisely.

11. I usually know my God-given agenda and can lead others in that direction.

12. I can adjust my leadership style to motivate a wide variety of people in the church to work together to meet a goal or accomplish the task at hand.

13. I don't always have to see the end result in my ministry activities as long as I know I'm caring for others.

14. If a brother or sister in Christ is hurting, I tell them what I think they want to hear in order to make both of us feel better.

15. I'm the kind of person who easily sees the right and wrong as it pertains to the eternal perspective in issues or situations.

16. When I discern that someone is acting out of selfish or unrighteous motives, I feel constrained to do something about it.

17. I find fulfillment by helping out the Body of Christ through simple hands-on kinds of tasks, such as building, sewing, fixing, cleaning, painting, preparing meals, etc.

18. When I see a practical need in the church, I want to personally meet the need quickly.

19. I am frustrated if there is not a structured environment in which I can educate others with the Biblical knowledge I've gained.

20. I believe learning Biblical truth requires diligence so I apply myself in ways such as note taking, outlining, and/or organizing ideas in order to better teach others.

21. While others may be discouraged at the slow growth of some believers, I welcome the opportunity to help them along.

22. While I believe in having goals and vision, I personally care more about how an individual is doing in their spiritual walk.

23. I am personally fulfilled when I give of myself through financial support even if others never know about it.

24. When it comes to the stewardship of God's resources, it bothers me if someone hasn't done their homework in order to get the best buy for their money.

25. While guiding others in God-given goals, I do it in such a way that they feel led of the Spirit.

26. It is important to me to list and/or chart out spiritual goals in an orderly fashion.

27. When I see people with mental/physical/emotional problems my heart is troubled causing me unrest until I've done something.

28. I carry a great weight in my heart when there is friction among believers (including myself).

29. I am extremely sensitive to the consequences of evil so I make conscious efforts to guard myself against temptation.

30. Because of my compulsion to identify truth in a situation, I can jump to conclusions that others feel are judgmental.

31. I am strongly drawn to focus on practical needs, not keying in as much to those needs that are spiritual.

32. I tend to jump right in to use my personal abilities and/or skills when a need arises within the church.

33. Studying Scripture is especially meaningful to me when I look at all the possible interpretations and angles.

34. When people make statements based solely on their personal feeling instead of facts about Biblical truth, it greatly bothers me.

35. I am motivated to discern why believers struggle and fail so I can help them grow in their walks.

36. It's not enough for me to share what I've learned from the scriptures. I need to know specifically how it is impacting others.

37. I feel very strongly about good financial stewardship which motivates me to help groups or individuals in this area.

38. When I see real need within the Body of Christ, I am compelled to reach out with my own resources to help.

39. I am able to clarify a God-given vision decisively and manage people or resources to fulfill it.

40. I enjoy directing people in ministries to accomplish a group's overall goals.

41. I believe church should be a place for healing, so if a brother or sister in Christ is hurting, I truly feel their pain with them.

42. I believe God has a time and place to say "No," but it's difficult for me if I think someone's feelings may be hurt.

43. In any relationship I have with another Christian, if I think it isn't based on openness and integrity, I must verbally confront the issue – I can't pretend things are okay when they are not.

44. When someone tells me of their struggle or need, I'm so caught up in discerning the why of it that I may not seem outwardly caring.

45. I don't feel I've demonstrated Christianity in action towards someone until I help them in a practical way.

46. In a church setting, I feel most comfortable working behind the scenes to help in whatever way is needed.

47. I must present the scriptural facts when I speak, preferring not to rely on stories or illustrations.

48. Studying and gaining Biblical knowledge on a wide range of topics is exciting. It really energizes me.

49. I can feel so intensely about helping someone grow in Christ that I may not realize when they don't want my help.

50. Instead of discerning underlying reasons for people's actions, I focus on strengthening and motivating them to take their spiritual walk more seriously.

51. Since I believe in the Biblical process of strategic planning in my personal budget, I believe others should be as diligent as I am.

52. Resourcefulness is a way of life for me because I want to support ministries that further the cause of Christ.

53. When I work with a group of believers, I am drawn to help them discern their created purpose and how to achieve it.

54. I am energized when brainstorming ideas for new ministries. I'm not overwhelmed by the multiple tasks at hand.

55. I am able to empathize with suffering people to the point I must involve myself in their healing process.

56. When I am confronted with situations where people are without eternal hope, such as people in prison, ill, or homeless, I can't get their suffering out of my mind.

57. I must speak the Biblical truth, even when I might be unpopular or look like the Lone Ranger.

58. In ministry groups or relationships, I am able to discern underlying issues or growth in others that I feel are critical to their effectiveness.

59. I take so much pleasure in helping others in the Body of Christ that I may tend to neglect personal or family responsibilities.

60. I am often willing to spend my own money to get a ministry-related job done if it means I can do it right away without red tape or planning restraints.

61. When I'm presented with a moral issue, I must do thorough Biblical research before drawing a conclusion.

62. I can be so preoccupied with the Scriptural details of what I have learned that I am often insensitive to what people see as their real needs.

63. Being a good listener isn't enough for me. I must help the person arrive at a Biblically-grounded solution to their problem.

64. It is not enough for me to help someone find out what is wrong – I want to walk with them, making sure the steps I lay out are taken seriously and with an eternal perspective.

65. It is important for me to know the money I give to the cause of Christ is wisely used.

66. I find greater pleasure in spending my resources on others who are working for the kingdom's sake rather than on myself.

67. I am able to effectively organize those in the Body of Christ, either on paper or in person, to achieve the goals that I perceive to be clearly God's plan.

68. I enjoy helping others evaluate their lives so they can formulate a plan to accomplish their spiritual goals.

69. If I see something going on in the church, I focus more on how people feel about it than the actual situation.

70. I believe God gave me the ability to empathize with people in order to get involved with those who are hurting.

71. I am compelled to confront lip service – people who say they believe something yet don't act on what they believe.

72. I feel strongly that wrong behavior must be dealt with, which causes me to challenge people as to the source of their behavior when I see it.

73. It satisfies me to do ministry-oriented tasks without being asked.

74. I have a stick with it attitude with respect to ministries that motivates me to get the job done.

75. When I hear an inspirational message, I am driven to know more of the critical detail and data behind it so I can study it further for myself.

76. I enjoy providing in-depth explanations clarifying information people have received concerning Scripture.

77. I am compelled to go beyond just identifying a moral or spiritual problem by helping find a meaningful solution.

78. I find myself bored and unfulfilled when I am not involved in personally guiding others in such a way as to see their lives change.

79. Knowing God's financial guidelines plays a critical part in my ability to influence others.

80. I take great pleasure in finding creative ways to give beyond my tithe.

81. It's important to me to stay focused spiritually when working with others.

82. When in a ministry role, I enjoy directing and/or overseeing others by challenging them to grow as they strive to meet individual and team goals.

83. I really value caring, compassion and gentleness. It is important to me that others see these Christ-like qualities in me.

84. I have a hard time confronting a brother or sister in Christ if I think it will hurt their feelings.

85. I feel so strongly about Biblical issues that I may speak sharply, offending those I'm speaking with.

86. I challenge believers to confront and turn from their sin, even in the face of my being rejected, pressured, or labeled narrow-minded.

87. I am frustrated when my schedule or current responsibilities hinder me from responding to a request for help from within the Church Body.

88. I consider it a privilege to assist others in their God-directed roles.

89. My love of learning about the Bible encourages others to want to study and learn as well.

90. I feel I must cover all planned aspects when making a Biblical point, often belaboring some point that may frustrate others.

91. When others face seemingly hopeless situations, I am driven to share scriptural avenues for change.

92. I thrive on knowing I have made a difference in someone's life through my Godly counsel or Godly encouragement.

93. I receive so many blessings through my financial giving that I wish everyone could experience the same thing.

94. I can't help but look for ways to impact the Lord's work through my resources.

95. When doing the Lord's work, bringing an administrative task or project to fruition is critical to me.

96. I love the challenge of inspiring a group of people to make a spiritual difference in the world.

97. When two people disagree on a Biblical matter, I feel sympathetic for both of them.

98. Sometimes it's hard for me to listen to Godly advice if it conflicts with what my heart tells me.

When you are finished with the questions, score each row going across. Then total each pair of rows (1 and 2), (3 and 4), etc., and put those totals in the far right hand column.

Now take the scoring key below and compare it to your totals on the survey sheet.

SCORING KEY FOR SPIRITUAL GIFTS	
Rows 1 and 2	PROPHECY
Rows 3 and 4	SERVICE
Rows 5 and 6	TEACHING
Rows 7 and 8	EXHORTATION
Rows 9 and 10	GIVING
Rows 11 and 12	LEADERSHIP
Rows 13 and 14	MERCY

The highest score is probably your **primary motivational** gift, but don't jump to a solid conclusion yet. This is only the first tool you will need to use in evaluating and discovering your **primary motivational** spiritual gift. Ideally, you will have one gift scoring visibly higher than the rest (by 5 points or more) and one gift scoring very low. The other five gifts ideally will fall somewhere in the middle.

However, if the spread between your highest and second highest score are less than 5 points, you may have a very strong **secondary motivational** gift too. I have seen this happen many times, mostly when a person has walked with the Lord and has been in ministry for quite awhile. When this is the case, I've seen that person take surveys years later, only to discover that the same two gifts are definitely the leading scores, but they flip-flop as to which is No. 1 and which is No. 2. I attribute this to the fact that a person's feelings may influence their answers somewhat at the time of the survey. Also, if you are presently in a ministry where you are using one of your gifts more than the other one, and both are your passion, one might be higher this time and the other one higher the next time. Ultimately, both are so close it is hard to be sure at times which one is the **primary** one.

On the other hand, if you have *two or three gifts* that are in close proximity to each other, then you will probably need further clarification. You may have a gift-mix. Some people get confused at this point, because their scores are so close.

Everyone will have a gift that scores the lowest. You would be wise to look at that gift, and ask the Lord to help you develop it over your lifetime. I believe God wants us balanced in every area of our lives. Your lowest scored gift indicates an area to really seek the Lord about. I often find that the prophetic person has the lowest scores in mercy. It is our responsibility to grow in the gifts as well as fruit of the Spirit.

On the next page is a chart for further clarifying your gift.

CHAPTER 12

Comparing and Contrasting the Motivational Gifts

Look at each gift listed below to see if the styles, objectives, and burdens fit your highest scored gift(s) on the survey. This is a second tool to confirm your **primary motivational gift.**

A "burden" is a spiritual weight or spiritual heaviness of soul. Ask yourself: "What is my style? When is my burden lifted?" As you compare the different gifts going across the page, you should be able to more closely confirm which gift is yours.

Prophecy	Service	Teaching	Exhortation	Giving	Leadership	Mercy
Style: Confrontational	Style: Serving	Style: Instructional/ educational	Style: Encouraging	Style: Gives $ and/or material items	Style: Ruling/ managing/ administrative/ oversight	Style: Compassionate
The gift of the prophecy aims at **to do**--wants to reform. They ask: "How did that person get there in the first place?" and declares "Let's get on with it."	The gift of service aims at the **practical need**.	The gift of teaching aims at the **mind**-- wants to educate. They ask: "How did it happen?" and "How can we prevent it?"	The gift of exhortation aims at the **heart**. They say: "Here's how to get out." And "Let's fix it."	The gift of giving aims at the **material and/or monetary needs**.	The gift of leadership aims at a **vision or concept**.	The gift of mercy aims at **feelings**.
Prophecy **proclaims** God's Point.	Service **helps** others in practical matters while they're moving from Point A to B.	Teaching **explains** God's Point.	Exhortation **encourages and gives specific action** to move from Point A to B.	**Giving** is often anonymous, especially if money.	Leadership **shares** God's vision or concept as if it is a reality.	Mercy **sympathizes and empathizes** with a person's hurt.
Their burden is lifted when the prophetic point is set forth as a Godly expectation and people are challenged to change.	Their burden is lifted when the practical need is met.	Their burden is lifted when God's point is clearly explained.	Their burden is lifted when they have shown you in an encouraging way how to get from Point A to B.	Their burden is lifted when the gift is received without making a big deal out of it. They don't feel comfortable if the recipient gushes.	Their burden is lifted when God's vision or concept becomes a reality.	Their burden is lifted when that hurt, problem, or need is gone.

By now you should have a pretty good idea of what your **primary motivational** spiritual gift is. It will be up to you to find a ministry where you can develop your gift. Ask the Holy Spirit to show you where to start. If you are presently ministering somewhere and it doesn't give you joy, ask the Lord if you need to refocus on a different ministry. He knows best, because He created you, and the gifts are really His to lend to each of His children. As you do, the key will be "Does exercising your gift give you joy **and also** bless others?"

Now, let's look at the **ministry** gifts.

SECTION 4

MINISTRY GIFTS

CHAPTER 13

Definition of the Ministry Gifts
Ephesians 4:11-12 and I Corinthians 12:28-30

Ministry Gifts: A God-appointed role or office within the church given to a believer to use for the equipping of the Body of Christ for ministry.

By their very function, these gifts have more potential to bring lasting fruit, as compared to the **manifestational** gifts. Ministry (service) will not become a burden or a burnout unless you are doing it in your own efforts. Once God gives you a heart for Him and a heart for people, this fruit will give you joy too. Ministry is where you have the ability to be creative. God will give you ideas, if you ask Him, about how to approach your very own God-designed ministry. Although every believer should be ministering as the Lord leads, not everyone's ministry will be defined by a formal role or office within their church. Some believers will willingly serve, because of a need in their church, out of their talents, abilities, or their **motivational or manifestational** gifts, but not necessarily out of one of the **ministry** gifts listed below. Do not let that lessen your desire to minister within the Body of Christ—instead let God be your guide as to how He wants to use you.

The Ministry Gifts are defined as follows:

Apostles (Ephesians 4:11 and I Corinthians 12:28-30)

Definition: One sent forth.

(I believe missionaries and church planters fit this category.)

Prophets (Ephesians 4:11 and I Corinthians 12:28-30)

Definition: One who is recognized by local, national, or international churches as either foretelling or mightily speaking forth God's Word calling people to conform to God's standards.

(This is also a **motivational** and **manifestational** gift exhibiting a different way of operating--for example, prophecy and prophetic utterances.)

Evangelists (Ephesians 4:11)

Definition: One who proclaims the salvation message.

(This gift does not necessarily mean an individual would have large numbers of converts. Consider Noah. He was an evangelist for 120 years, a "preacher of righteousness" (II Peter 2:5), but was only able to save himself and his immediate family. Many missionaries labor for years but do not see mass conversions; many do not even see individuals accept Christ, but they are evangelists nonetheless.)

Pastors/Teachers (combined in Ephesians 4:11)

Definition: One who oversees a group of believers and teaches God's Word in a formal or structured setting.

(When combined as in this passage, the pastor is to be the main teacher of God's Word. A teacher is not always a pastor, but a pastor must be able to teach.)

Teacher (individually in I Corinthians 12:28)

Definition: One who teaches God's Word in a formal or structured setting.

(An arena for teaching can be 1-on-1 or in a group setting. It can include discipleship.)

(Teaching is also a **motivational** gift that can be developed into a **ministry** role.)

Miracles (I Corinthians 12:28-30)

Definition: One who is recognized by local, national, or international churches as one who performs miracles.

(In some churches this is an office or role recognized by that church, because the Lord has raised up someone in their own body. It is equally important to remember that all miracles are from God, and the person performing them is simply a vessel.)

(Working of miracles also falls under the category of **manifestational** gifts.)

Gifts of Healing (I Corinthians 12:28-30)

Definition: One who is recognized by local, national, or international churches as one who performs healings.

(As with working of miracles, in some churches this is an office or role recognized by that church, because the Lord has raised up someone in their own body. Again, let's remember that all gifts of healing are from God, and the person performing them is simply a vessel.

(Gifts of healing also fall under the category of **manifestational** gifts.)

Helps (I Corinthians 12:28-30)

Definition: This is the only time helps is listed in the Bible as a gift. It means "to aid" in Greek[1]. It refers especially to relief towards the poor, orphaned, widowed, or stranger by practical service.

(I believe this church office is the **ministry** gift umbrella that includes service, giving, and hospitality.)

(As a **ministry** gift in many churches, this gift would be considered the office of a Deacon, for example a practical activity based on actions not words.)

(Service and giving are also **motivational** gifts with a different way of operating, because each one ministers to the practical needs of <u>all</u>, not just the poor, orphaned, widow, or stranger.)

---

[1] *Strong's Concordance*

Governments (I Corinthians 12:28-30)

Definition: This gift is sometimes called "administration" which means "to steer" in Latin[1] and includes organizing paperwork and people.

(I believe this church office is the **ministry** gift umbrella for both the gifts of administration [which refers to paperwork] and leadership [which refers to ruling and guiding people]).

(Leadership [ruling in KJV] is also a **motivational** gift that may develop into a governing or administrative role within the church.)

Tongues (I Corinthians 12:28-30)

Definition: A God-created language exercised by the speaker that has not been acquired naturally, studied, or learned.

(In some churches this **ministry** gift is recognized as being a specific office, and is usually exercised as part of a prayer or prophetic ministry.)

(Tongues are also a **manifestational** gift used in one's private prayer life, and some people refer to it as their prayer language.)

Discovering your Ministry Gifts

The best way to discover your **ministry** gift is to follow God's unique guidance by stepping out in faith, and begin serving in your church in an area where you can use your **motivational** gift.

Perhaps you are in a small group, and as you step out and use your gift, others will begin to notice and tell you how blessed they are because of something you said or did. In reality you will be using that special gift, but they may or may not recognize it for what it is (a spiritual gift). They might just see it as a need or position being filled. That's unfortunate, but you will be so blessed using your gift, it should not matter to you. Just be sure to give God the credit (glory).

If your pastor is knowledgeable about spiritual gifts, you might go to him, tell him you believe you know what your spiritual gift is, and ask him where it could be used in your church. As you step out by serving, you may find that your **motivational** gift will also become a **ministry** gift.

The more you let God use you, the more you will become comfortable with your gift. An overflowing joy should accompany its use. Affirmation from others goes a long way, but if you still do not have a passion for the specific ministry you are in, and experience little joy, perhaps you are not in a ministry that fits you and your gift. If that is the case, pray for guidance from God and try another ministry. Over and over I have discovered that when people have accurately identified their **primary motivational** gift, they find abundant joy in their chosen ministry.

As you are ministering, you need to ask God to give you spiritual eyes and spiritual ears to see Him working. It is then you will more easily catch a glimpse of God expressing Himself through you with the **manifestational** gifts.

---

[1] *Strong's Concordance*

CHAPTER 14

Conclusion

Years ago, I also heard Pastor Chuck Smith say that one of his life's main prayers was that God would keep him usable.[1] "Such wisdom" I thought, and I decided right then and there to make that my life's prayer too.

In hindsight, this letter has turned into a book. Even though I have many more life stories and could continue sharing more about the gifts, I simply had to stop. It is my prayer for you that God would keep you useable. I pray that would include rich experiences with the spiritual gifts throughout your life too.

In a nutshell, let's review how the gifts might be developed in your life:

First you take the Survey to discover or confirm your **motivational gift.** →

↘

Then as you exercise your **ministry gift** God develops it. →

↘

As you are developing your **motivational gift** in ministry, the Lord will surprise you with a **manifestational gift.**

On His Word, I promise!!

---

[1] Chuck Smith, http://blueletterbible.org/Comm/chuck_smith_sn/Act/Act28.html. Online posting as of 8/11/06.

www.ingramcontent.com/pod-product-compliance
Lightning Source LLC
LaVergne TN
LVHW081359060426
835510LV00016B/1899